Stuff

Stuff

Daniel Miller

polity

Contents

Acknowledgements

I have always felt that a subject called Social Anthropology could manage to be a hell of a lot more social than is commonly the case. As a result, I changed my way of working many years ago. Increasingly I carry out almost all my research in collaboration. This means that, although this book is largely about my research, it presents results and ideas that have, in most cases, been developed only through my engagement with others. It is impossible, for example, to consider my discussion of the sari in chapter 1 without this being also credited simultaneously to Mukulika Banerjee, or that of the Jamaican mobile phone without this being equally seen as the work of Heather Horst. Other research collaborators have included Zuzana Búriková for the work on au pairs, Alison Clarke for the work on shopping, Mirca Madianou for the work on long-distance relationships, Lucy Norris for the work on clothing and waste, Fiona Parrott for the work on loss, Don Slater for the work on the Internet in Trinidad, and Sophie Woodward for the work on denim.

One of the other delights of my work has been the collaboration with students and especially with PhD students. This creates a vicarious pride which is not entirely dissimilar from that of parents and children. As in the latter case, it is often the younger party that shows much more maturity than the older. Many years ago I established something we call a dinner/drinking group, which meets monthly to drink, discuss pre-circulated papers by the students and then eat (and occasionally party). Sometimes in each other's homes, sometimes in my office, sometimes in restaurants.

Thanks to this format, friendships have often been formed, and also collaborative publications. The publications in turn reflect the cross-influence between what often started as quite different projects. This has made it easier to produce edited collections with relative coherence compared to most such volumes. So I owe a considerable amount to past and present PhD students: Ivana Bajic, Ira Berdichevsky, Julie Botticello, Achsah Carrier, Pat Clark, Alison Clarke, Magda Craciun, Dimitrios Dalakaglou, Inge Daniels, Adam Drazin, Justin Finden-Crofts, Pauline Garvey, Cleo Gougoulis, Martha Guarneros, Anat Hecht, Heather Horst, Gabrielle Hosein, Neil Jarman, Mark Johnson, Emma Lindblad, Tom McDonald, Desmond Mallikarachichi, Simone Mangal, Jean-Sébastien Marcoux, Marjorie Murray, Razvan Nicolescu, Kaori O'Connor, Bodil Olesen (honorary), Panarai Ostapirat, Andrea Pellegram, Anna Pertiera, Elia Petridou, Sigrid Rausing, Tom Rogers, Ed Ross, Florian Schlichting, Miran Shin, Andrew Skuse, Jo Tacchi, Chang-Kwo Tan, Sophie Woodward. In addition, over the years there have been constant visitors, students who came for just a few months, who joined this group, and then left again; I simply cannot mention all these and I hope they will forgive me. Others who have commented on this manuscript include Eleana Yalouri and Karen Ida Dannesboe as well as anonymous reviewers.

I also owe a considerable debt to my colleagues over the years in material culture studies at University College London. That is, Barbara Bender, Victor Buchli, Paolo Favero, John Gledhill, Suzanne Küchler, Chris Pinney, Michael Rowlands, Chris Tilley and Graeme Ware. I have only ever worked at UCL and never once been tempted by any other potential job. There are also many colleagues around the world who have encouraged and inspired me from time to time, and helped especially when I was first developing these ideas, for example, Rob Foster, Nicky Gregson, Caroline Humphrey, Webb Keane, Marilyn Strathern, Nicholas Thomas and Rick Wilk. As well as others, sadly deceased, such as Judy Attfield, Alfie Gell and Marianne Gullestad.

On a more personal note, of particular importance has been the friendship and advice over the years of Mukulika Banerjee,

Kathryn Earle and Stephen Frosh. Nothing I do has ever been possible without the support of Rickie, Rachel and David and I would like to thank Rickie, in particular, for her assistance in editing the text. Finally I am indebted to a vast number of people who have granted me such generous help during fieldwork in a dozen different countries over many many years. I can't name them but it is their ideas and actions that inform this book.

Prologue: My Life as an Extremist

Don't, just don't, ask for or expect a clear definition of 'stuff'. Sure, there are academic traditions that believe knowledge is best conveyed through such clear definitions. This is perhaps essential in the natural sciences. But personally I have always had a horror of what I think of as pedantic semantics. To try and determine the exact criteria by which some things would be excluded from *stuff* as perhaps less tangible, or too transient, would be a hopeless exercise. Does an email or a fashion count as stuff, a kiss or a leaf or polystyrene packing? This is a book about the variety of things that we might term stuff, but nowhere in this volume will you find any attempt at a definition of that term. Rather it is intended to introduce my own perspective on the study of material culture, a set of studies that are principally concerned with stuff. Material culture is no better defined than stuff is. In practice these studies have promiscuously picked up on interesting topics and perspectives that more self-absorbed, well-defined sub-disciplines felt were outside of their brief. Material culture thrives as a rather undisciplined substitute for a discipline: inclusive, embracing, original, sometimes quirky researches and observations.

Material culture starts, after all, with mere happenstance: the history of the established academic disciplines. Some of these seem obvious; we have language and so we have linguistics. Others on reflection seem a trifle bizarre. The study of rocks is allocated to geography, and then somehow the study of traffic gets mixed into the pot. Yet no one thought to have an academic discipline whose specific area of study would be artefacts, the object world created by humanity. It could so easily have been otherwise. Consider the degree to which established academic disciplines, from archaeology to architecture, from sociology to design, require theories and perspectives on this material world. If material culture had existed for a century of established study in thousands of colleges, it would have been as taken for granted as linguistics is today. But this didn't happen and it is not the purpose of this book to create a discipline where there wasn't one. Instead it seeks to welcome this aberration; to embrace the openness and collegiality of not having to be overly disciplined. *Stuff* as a term serves just fine. Not establishing a discipline doesn't mean that a study of stuff lacks substance or consequence. Material culture studies are becoming recognized as a vital contribution to half a dozen established disciplines, from archaeology to design. We provide many theories, and analytical approaches, for example, in discussing the specific nature and consequences of materiality. Several of these are discussed in the course of this book.

This volume is not a textbook, nor a systematic review of the range of studies of material culture. Most of that work is barely mentioned here. It is instead, together with a future companion volume, intended as a retrospective examination of my own previous research. When I was first approached by a publisher to consider creating an edited collection based on my previously published work, I was ambivalent. I had always felt that, in some respects, such collections are lacking something. In general, an edited collection requires very little effort, partly because one is not required to re-think earlier material in the light of later work, while as soon as a book appears in press I tend to see only its deficiencies. Fortunately such introspections are limited by the fact that I write mainly as an anthropologist. This means that most of my writing is about something far more interesting than myself or my ideas – it is an account of other peoples, their practices and cosmologies and ideas. As accounts of others they hopefully have just as much to teach now as when I first wrote them, which helps give me confidence in the value of a return to these works. But I still preferred not to create a book of edited papers, but to wait until I could partially rewrite this past corpus. By reconsidering each publication in the light of others I could draw attention to some larger themes that connect them, and longer trajectories that they developed over time. With twenty-six previous volumes this task seemed better divided into two main themes.

Other grounds for this rewriting of earlier work emerge in retrospect. Academia, as the anthropologist Bourdieu points out, in its structure of employment, creates an incentive for each generation to attempt the overthrow of its predecessors, demonstrating the intellectual agility of the young by repudiating established arguments. As a student in Cambridge, in a highly competitive environment, this desire to demonstrate cleverness, as opposed to understanding, was paramount. Amongst my first works, a jointly edited collection called *Ideology, Power and Prehistory*[1] was a critique of Foucault. There was a need to demonstrate that I was comfortable with the work of figures such as Derrida and Lacan and clever enough to appropriate the opaque and often recondite terms and ideas that impressed, partly through obfuscating phraseology. I gained a great deal from that lively competition and ambition. But it has also taken me a considerable time to overcome the more negative aspects of that legacy: to appreciate that a discipline such as anthropology, devoted to the comprehension and welfare of people in society, was ultimately served much better by understanding than by cleverness, which merely betrayed the need to express the stories and suffering of others. The intention was that this book would attempt to retain some of these insights from earlier work, but to release them from the encrusting jargon in which they were first written and instead to try and convey them as clearly as possible. Another problem with an edited collection is its selectivity. By contrast, a re-composed retrospective examination allows one in hindsight to consider the corpus of work more holistically. So this volume seeks both to juxtapose and to relate theories of stuff, applied anthropology, ethnographic reportage and the analysis of particular genres of clothing, home and the media. Ultimately there are a good many reasons why you should give a stuff about stuff, and this book attempts to bring them together.

For all these reasons, I approached Polity Press with the idea of doing something rather different from a conventional edited volume: to write two new books that summarized and reviewed my own work in a clearer, less pretentious style that could examine my academic trajectory as a whole. This first volume speaks to around a dozen books and over a hundred papers about material culture. All this research was undertaken under the auspices of, and using the methodologies of, the discipline of anthropology. It is therefore a complement to other material culture work orientated more to disciplines such as design or philosophy.[2] It is also very much beholden to the specific context of the department of Anthropology at University College London, from where all this research was conducted. My own research has occupied a specific niche within an ecological diversity of ideas that colonize other feeding grounds for material culture, grazed by my colleagues in the department. These include the anthropology of art, museum studies and culture heritage management, visual anthropology, and the anthropology of landscape and architecture. Our collectivity is represented in the *Journal of Material Culture* which we edit, and many other publications. I also run a blog at www.materialworldblog.com with colleagues at UCL and other universities. While this volume represents almost entirely my own work, rather than that of the larger group, I am happy to acknowledge the extent to which my research has constantly been informed by my colleagues. It is even more influenced by over forty PhD students, some of whose work is discussed here.

This book is intended as an interim report rather than a signing off. I have recently started several new projects on topics ranging from global denim to the use of media by migrants for the conduct of long-distance relationships. Hopefully consolidation can create a higher academic platform for the launch of future work. But the foundation is constructed from the building blocks of material culture itself. The central argument of this book is a paradox: that the best way to understand, convey and appreciate our humanity is through attention to our fundamental materiality. It might seem that this would only be true of our particular present – a consequence of the sheer scale of contemporary consumption and its implications for environmental and other ethical debates. I do not believe this to be the case. I will argue that non-industrial societies are just as much material cultures as we are. This volume treats consumer and non-consumer societies equally and in juxtaposition. A consideration of the specific issues of consumer society will be the subject of a second retrospective volume entitled *Consumed by Doubt*. If discussion of issues of political economy, indeed politics more generally, including a concern for the consequences of materialism for the future of the environment, are largely missing from this volume, it is because they are the subject of this second complementary work. Before that more political debate, however, I feel we need to consider the more foundational issues: the consequences of our materiality and of material culture for a more profound understanding of what we ourselves are.

The leitmotif of this book is a challenge to our common-sense opposition between the person and the thing, the animate and inanimate, the subject and the object. Certainly this is being achieved in some measure these days through science. New forms of biomedicine constantly challenge the way we think about such matters as the body and perception. Anthropologists including Donna Harraway, Emily Martin, Marilyn Strathern and Bruno Latour have considered these consequences of science, especially biomedical discoveries, as well as the languages and images we use to convey them. Here, by contrast, I am concerned with developments in social science, rather than natural science; with anthropology's qualitative encounter with the diversity of peoples, and the increasing diversity of things.

Stuff is ubiquitous, and problematic. But whatever our environmental fears or concerns over materialism, we will not be helped by either a theory of stuff, or an attitude to stuff, that simply tries to oppose ourselves to it; as though the more we think of things as alien, the more we keep ourselves sacrosanct and pure. The idea that stuff somehow drains away our humanity, as we dissolve into a sticky mess of plastic and other commodities, is really an attempt to retain a rather simplistic and false view of pure and prior unsullied humanity. There are good uses of anthropology and also terrible uses of anthropology. One of the latter is a primitivism which assumes that because tribal people didn't have much stuff they were necessarily less materialistic. On the contrary, some of the most sophisticated relationships to things may be found amongst peoples such as Australian Aboriginals or North West Coast American Indians, whose material possessions may seem paltry, compared to modern Londoners'.

Furthermore, not having things is no evidence that you don't want them. An Amazonian Indian may be much more desirous of possessions than we are, but simply unable to obtain them. The anthropologist Stephen Hughes-Jones, who spent many years in

Amazonian research, was shocked by the avaricious desire to obtain goods that he encountered amongst people who up to then had almost no possessions.[3] It may not be what pop groups want us to believe of the peoples of Amazonia, but personally I turn to pop groups for music rather than for anthropology. Anyway, why should we deprive Amazonian Indians of the delights of pop music? This model of the noble, unmaterialistic savage is entirely unhelpful. All it achieves is an assumption of lost purity. It makes us feel alienated and polluted simply for being who we are. Instead, this book tries to face up to stuff: to acknowledge it, respect it and expose ourselves to our own materiality rather than to deny it. My starting point is that we too are stuff, and our use and identification with material culture provides a capacity for enhancing, just as much as for submerging, our humanity. My hope and intention is that this book will demonstrate how and why a more profound appreciation of things will lead to a more profound appreciation of persons.

For some time now I have had the ambition to become an extremist, something I consider to be a noble ambition, at least for an anthropologist. In fact being an extremist more or less sums up what I mean by being an anthropologist. While I am generally rather unsympathetic to disciplinary labels and work in collaboration with wonderful researchers from many other disciplines, I am committed to what I see as this extremist quality in anthropology. But, at this point, I suppose I had better explain why I would consider extremism, in this particular context, to be such a noble pursuit. I would think that one of the less controversial characterizations one could make about the modern world is that it shows an ever increasing tendency to greater particularity and simultaneously to greater universality. On the one hand there is a proliferation of diversity in occupations, in commodities, in experiences and in relationships. A Londoner might work in corporate PR or waste incineration, play with a Nintendo Wii or beach volleyball, and love karaoke or tequila. At the same time we devise institutions based on implied universals, such as children's rights, web technology, neo-liberalism, or a curriculum for chemistry, that have the ambition of reaching all the peoples of the world. At one end of the spectrum we become ever more particular as individuals in our work, tastes, practices and interests. At the other end we have recourse to ever more universal aspirations, some of which we subscribe to, but most of which do not depend on our active identification. Most, such as human rights or medical services, grow more in the form of institutions that strive for universality in practice. Of course, these two processes are connected. Institutions are more universal the more they encompass an increasing particularity.

This simultaneous growth in particularity and universality is one way of defining the modern world. It was central to that philosophical tradition which is usually called dialectics and is most closely associated with the work of Hegel, a philosophical foundation I will refer to several times in this volume, since it is the one which underpins much of my own work. How should academics respond to this condition? I find that, in general, most disciplines respond by searching out some kind of middle ground. Any social science or natural science of the person, such as psychology, that proceeds through hypothesis testing will tend to focus upon some small element of predictability. It will propose a theory or analysis that can be tested against a relatively limited and often controlled observation. In applying for a research grant most academics will present an argument based on a quite immediate relationship between a particular behaviour and a specific generalization or cause. Is class or ethnicity better correlated to educational performance in the UK? How do older people in Chicago respond when you look them in the eye directly or look at them indirectly? Do Serbians more often consider that they are infected with a cold when the weather is cold?

The anthropology I am committed to eschews such hypothesis testing. My problem in seeking research grants is that invariably my only real hypothesis is that I really have very little idea of what I am actually going to find when I go out to conduct fieldwork. This hypothesis has always proved correct. In going to live within another community I assume that the most important findings are going to be about things one didn't even suspect existed before going to live there. If you didn't know they existed, how could you have hypothesized about them? In my experience an inconsistent, opportunistic research student tends to be far more original and productive than consistent research students, who achieve merely what they set out to do.

I don't then follow this search for the middle ground of academic research – the testing ground. This is because I see the primary purpose of anthropology as fulfilling an ideal I derive originally from Hegel. The central problem confronted by the modern world is that universalism and particularity can so easily lose touch with each other. Finance, theory or aspirations to be good can all take on a universalistic abstract form. But these then fall out of synch with the actual diversity, complexity and contradictions of business, analysis and the ethics of the everyday. So the purpose of anthropology is to bring these two back into conversation with and acknowledgement of each other. After all, there is probably no discipline as committed to particularism as anthropology. A principle of its work is relativism. We conduct fieldwork by spending a year participating in the lives of members of an Apostolic church in Zimbabwe, rice farmers of North West Thailand, separated Filipino families, or aspiring pop bands in Manchester. We are not supposed to claim authority to write about these communities until we have thoroughly immersed ourselves in the everyday life of these very specific groups. Our methodology, known as ethnography, typically consists of living with families for a year or more, speaking their language and participating in mundane activities such as cooking and cleaning.

This is a world apart from those who are satisfied with questionnaires and focus groups and seek to conduct experiments. Anthropologists can become so extreme that all generalization seems suspect. Yes, this Balinese family used a word we might translate as love, but the people in the next valley use it slightly differently, as do women as against men, or younger as against older women. Indeed on reflection they seem to be using it a bit differently this year from last year. So how could we ever say what that word love means to a people we drastically overgeneralize every time we use the term Balinese? Such extreme relativism seems doomed to extreme parochialism, a common affliction amongst anthropologists.

Yet, at the very same time, anthropology is a discipline dedicated to universals, and will continually throw up ideas such as Lévi-Strauss's structuralism, the principle of the gift, anthropological versions of Marxism or psychoanalysis, relationships as negotiated experience, the consequences of our materiality. Our theories seem to transcend all such particularities. Culture itself is viewed as binary, or founded in exchange or in kinship, or opposed to nature. We attempt to write a book about *stuff*. Some of our generalizations are so vast they are scary. The advantage of this simultaneous commitment to the extremes of particularity and of generality is that anthropology can make its major contribution to the understanding of humanity through constantly re-connecting these two without losing a commitment to both extremes. In that sense this discipline that many people regard as looking backwards to prior manifestations of humanity is actually uniquely geared to the central dilemmas of modern life.

Most commonly, good anthropological work reveals the particular as a manifestation of the universal. So there is regional neo-liberalism. Coca-Cola is everywhere, but means slightly different things in each locality. The gift is based on an obligation to return the gift but this works differently within the Chinese *Guanxi* system than with the Maori *Hau*. My colleague Mukulika Banerjee is an expert on democracy. She has researched why people bother to vote in an Indian village. But this in turn means understanding how these villages respond to the universal pretensions of democracy as an ideal. Democracy as a practice and as a consequence varies from place to place, and yet cannot be understood without also acknowledging its authority as a global aspiration or global conceit. Perhaps there is no capitalism, only capitalisms. So the reason I desire to be an extremist is that this represents a commitment to keep in touch simultaneously with the extremes of universalism and particularism in modern life.

Why does this matter so much? It is because one of the major dangers that besets the world today lies in the increasing dissociation of the two extremes. The universals fly apart from the particular. Economists, psychologists and human rights lawyers come up with more and more general models that claim to represent humanity and assume increasing authority to be imposed upon humanity as a whole. All economies are increasingly expected to seek to accord with ever more abstract, often mathematical models that generate new financial instruments. All children are supposed now to have the same basic human rights. But these universals become detached from the very specifics of our humanity and cultural differences that remain meaningful. London may be gloriously cosmopolitan, but the devout Sikh remains very distinct from the retro-Goth living next door. So I subscribe to a discipline that is prepared to dedicate a year in order to know what it means to live as a devout Sikh, but equally what it means to live as a retro-Goth in London; to simultaneously consider the implications of neo-liberalism and universal human rights. But then there is always a third stage to this dialectic without which our task remains incomplete. This is to ask what the consequences of neo-liberalism are to the retro-Goth and the challenge a devout Sikh might represent to assumptions about universal human rights. Only at that point have we achieved the goal of being anthropologists.

Once upon a time anthropologists were associated only with the study of less developed or small-scale societies. I hope those days are gone forever. All people today are equal in their right to the burden of being studied by some or other anthropologist. My definition of the anthropologist is someone who seeks to demonstrate the consequences of the universal for the particular and of the particular for the universal by equal devotion to the empathetic understanding and encompassment of both. This is why I believe my extremism to be a noble cause. But it follows from this same premise that I have, within this universalistic ambition, my own particularism. My particular particularism is the field of material culture – the study of stuff.

This book charts a path towards material culture studies through several chapters, each of which takes responsibility for providing a different perspective upon this endeavour. The first chapter on clothing is a demolition of the most common academic and popular view of stuff – the idea that objects signify or represent us and that they are principally signs or symbols that stand for persons. Instead, I argue that in many respects stuff actually creates us in the first place. More specifically, I demonstrate why clothing is not superficial. The second chapter presents theories of material culture. Starting with a theory of objects per se, it moves steadily upwards to the more rarefied theory of objectification and thence to a plane of transcendence where we gain a perspective from which we can no longer distinguish subjects from objects. It then examines the consequences of our various beliefs about the properties of materiality itself. The third chapter takes these neat and clean abstract theories and drags them back down to the messy world of application in its consideration of our relationship with our homes and houses. It literally domesticates such theories through examining the process of 'accommodating', and reveals how such theories, when applied to specifics, have to incorporate wider factors such as the impact of governments, the history of styles, international migration, and the power and agency that lies in the houses themselves.

The fourth chapter examines the ambiguous materiality of media and communication. Stuff is not necessarily a thing we can hold or touch. This chapter also takes responsibility for issues not previously addressed, but which emerge in applied anthropology. What can and should we do with the knowledge and understanding gained by material culture studies, when it comes to the welfare of populations? How can we hope to improve their conditions and respect their aspirations while considering the negative impact of their desires? Finally, in the fifth chapter, we consider stuff as the matter of life and death; that which brings us into the world and that which helps us part from the world. In this final chapter I take what was introduced theoretically as the way objects construct subjects, and show how this is true for the everyday understanding of what it means to be human.

1

Why Clothing is not Superficial

When I began my career as an academic, committed to the study of material culture, the dominant theory and approach to the study of things was that of semiotics. We were taught that the best way to appreciate the role of objects was to consider them as signs and as symbols that represent us. The example that was most commonly employed to illustrate this perspective was that of clothing, since it seemed intuitively obvious that we choose clothing for precisely this reason. My clothing shows that I am sexy, or Slovenian, or smart, or all three. Through the study of the differentiation of clothing we could embark upon the study of the differentiation of us.[1] Clothes might represent gender differences, but also class, levels of education, cultures of origin, confidence or diffidence, our occupational roles as against our evening leisure. Clothing was a kind of pseudo-language that could tell us about who we are. As such, material things were a neglected adjunct to the study of language: an apparently unspoken form of communication that could actually speak volumes once we had attuned ourselves to this capacity. Anthropological discussions by Mary Douglas and Marshall Sahlins, amongst others, that advocated this approach seemed to suggest a whole new significance to the study of stuff.

There is no doubt that material culture studies was significantly enhanced by the arrival of this semiotic perspective; but ultimately it became as much a limitation as an asset. This chapter aims to repudiate a semiotic approach to things in general and to clothing in particular. Consider one of the best-known clothing stories. 'The Emperor's New Clothes' is a morality tale about pretentiousness and vanity. The Emperor is persuaded by his tailors that the clothes they have stitched him are fine to the point of invisibility, leaving him to strut naked around his court. The problem with semiotics is that it makes the clothes into mere servants whose task it is to represent an Emperor – the human subject. Clothes do our bidding and represent us to the outside world. In themselves, clothes are pretty worthless creatures, superficial, of little consequence, mere inanimate stuff. It is the Emperor, the self, that gives them such dignity, glamour and refinement.

But what and where is this self that the clothes represent? In both philosophy and everyday life we imagine that there is a real or true self which lies deep within us. On the surface is found the clothing which may represent us and may reveal a truth about ourselves, but it may also lie. It is as though if we peeled off the outer layers we would finally get to the real self within. But what was revealed by the absence of clothes was not the Emperor's inner self but his outward conceit. Actually, as Ibsen's Peer Gynt observed, we are all onions. If you keep peeling off our layers you find – absolutely nothing left. There is no true inner self. We are not Emperors represented by clothes, because if we remove the clothes there isn't an inner core. The clothes were not superficial, they actually were what made us what we think we are. At first this sounds odd, unlikely, implausible or just plain wrong. To discover the truth of Peer Gynt, as applied to clothing, we need to travel to Trinidad, from there to India, and then to use these experiences to re-think our relationship to clothing back in London.

Trinidad[2]

The problem with viewing clothing as the surface that represents, or fails to represent, the inner core of true being is that we are then inclined to consider people who take clothes seriously as themselves superficial. Prior to feminism, newspaper cartoons had few qualms in showing women as superficial merely by portraying their desire to shop for shoes or dresses. Young black males were superficial because they wanted expensive trainers that they were not supposed to be able to afford. By contrast, we student academics at places such as Cambridge were deep and profound because frankly we looked rubbish, and clearly didn't much care that we did. When I met my wife as fellow students, my trousers were held up at the top with string and their hem at the base with staples. She must have thought I was deep, because there certainly wasn't much to attract her on the surface. Such assumptions are fine within the confines of Cambridge but a problem for an anthropologist going out to Trinidad. Because the point of anthropology is to enquire empathetically into how other people see the world. Dismissing them as superficial would represent a rather disastrous start to such an exercise. For Trinidadians in general were devoted to clothes, and knew they were good at looking good. Colourful prints and butterfly belts were a priority.

I worked much of my time in Trinidad with squatters who had neither a water supply nor electricity in the house. Yet women living in these squatters' camps might have a dozen or twenty pairs of shoes. A common leisure activity was to hold a fashion display, on a temporary catwalk, along one of the open spaces within the squatters' encampment. They would beg, borrow, make or steal clothes. It wasn't just the clothes, it was also the hair, the accessories and the way they strutted their stuff; knowing how to walk sexy and to look glamorous or beguiling. Movements were based on an exaggerated self-confidence and a strong eroticism, with striding, bouncy, or dance-like displays. In local parlance there should be something *hot* about the clothing and something *hot* about the performance. On evenings I could spend three hours with them, waiting as they got themselves ready to go out and party, trying on and discarding outfits until they got it right.

This association is hardly new for the region. Early accounts of slave society in the Caribbean include references to the particular devotion of slaves to clothing. A. C. Carmichael stated in 1833: 'Generally speaking, the coloured women have an insatiable passion for showy dresses and jewels . . . The highest class of females dress more showily and far more expensively than European ladies'.[3] Freilich, carrying out ethnographic research in an impoverished village in 1957–8, reports, 'the wife of one of the peasants said "every new function needs new clothes. I would not wear the same dress to two functions in the same district"'.[4] This

desire was still more forcefully expressed during the 1970s oil
boom in Trinidad when both seamstresses and their clients suggested that purchasing two new outfits a week was quite common
for women in work. We do not necessarily condemn a population
just because they show some devotion to stuff. Anthropologists
celebrate, rather than demean, the devotion of Trobriand Islanders
to canoe prows or of the Nuer to cattle. But curiously a devotion
to clothing, as one can see from these descriptions by outsiders,
was always viewed rather more harshly, especially for those
without wealth.

As evident in the description of the local catwalk, what mostly
concerned Trinidadians was not *fashion* – that is, the collective
following of a trend, but *style* – that is, the individual construction
of an aesthetic based not just on what you wear, but on how you
wear it. There used to be a term *saga boys* for men who combined
sartorial originality with ways of walking and talking that never
let up from conspicuous display. Another local term *gallerying*
gets it just right. Trinidad style, in turn, has two components,
individualism and transience. The individual has to re-combine
elements in their own way. The source of these elements is unim-
portant. They may be copied from the soap operas or the fashion
shows which appear on television, sent from relatives abroad or
purchased while abroad. They may simply re-combine local products. But the various elements should work together, be appropriate to the person who carries them off well, for ideally just one
particular occasion. It didn't matter what clothes cost or even
whether the clothes worn on the catwalk belonged to them or
were borrowed for the occasion. This wasn't about accumulation,
but about transience. The stylist may learn from fashion but only
as the vanguard. Then they must move on. Trinidad's best known
cultural export, Carnival, enshrines this transience. Individuals
may spend weeks, if not months, creating elaborate and time-
consuming costumes. But these must be discarded and re-made
annually. What is celebrated is the event, the moment.

There are many possible reasons why Trinidadians might
have developed this affinity with style as individual and transient
expression. Some theories go back to slavery and beyond. Henry
Lewis Gates in his book *The Signifying Monkey* argued for a West
African aesthetic structure found especially amongst the Yoruba.[5]
He notes the way jazz musicians take up themes and develop them,

but very often return to a pastiche of well-known rhythms and tunes from previous compositions. In ordinary speech both musicians and others will refer to *Signifyin(g)* upon someone or something. One can see a similar use of clothing in the development of *vogueing* made famous by Madonna and the film *Paris is Burning*, which treats clothing and high fashion in a similar referential manner. But Trinidadian clothing style doesn't return to classic themes in this way.

An alternative might be to look, not to some origin in Africa, but to the experience of slavery itself. The idea of keeping things on the surface as a defensive strategy against the condition of extreme degradation is brilliantly depicted by Toni Morrison in her novel *Beloved*: 'so you protected yourself and loved small. Picked the tiniest stars out of the sky to own . . . Anything bigger wouldn't do. A woman, a child, a brother – a big love that would split you wide open in Alfred Georgia.'[6] The precarious existence given by the condition of slavery precluded any internalization of love, since there was no knowing when this love-object might be wrested away, resulting in a kind of adaptive tendency to keep things on the surface, to refuse any internalization and thus to minimize one's sense of loss. This is more plausible, and may remain relevant to many of those in the squatting area. But the majority of the population of Trinidad do not have origins in Africa and slavery. Many come from South Asia or have mixed backgrounds.

So, instead of trying to ask where such a relationship to style comes from, instead of seeing it as a problem that requires explanation, we can turn the lens back onto ourselves. Why do we think that a devotion to clothing is a problem anyway? Why do we see it as a sign of superficiality and what does the very term superficiality imply? The problem with a theory of semiotics and of treating clothing as superficial is that we presume a certain relationship between the interior and the exterior. We possess what could be called a *depth ontology*. The assumption is that *being* – what we truly are – is located deep inside ourselves and is in direct opposition to the surface. A clothes shopper is shallow because a philosopher or a saint is deep. The true core to the self is relatively constant and unchanging and also unresponsive to mere circumstance. We have to look deep inside ourselves to find ourselves. But these are all metaphors. Deep inside ourselves is blood and bile, not philosophical certainty. We won't find a soul by cutting deep into someone, though I suppose we might accidentally release it. My point is that there is simply no reason on earth why another population should see things this same way. No reason at all why they should consider our real being to be deep inside and falsity on the outside. The argument here is that Trinidadians by and large don't.

In stark contrast to this depth ontology Trinidadians seem to have almost a horror of things becoming interiorized, rather than kept on the surface. Perhaps the most popular leisure activity in Trinidad is the *lime*, in which a group of people either hang around a street corner or travel in a group, for example, into the countryside to *make a cook*. A feature of the lime is the genre of verbal insult which is known as *picong* or giving *fatigue*. The individual failings of a fellow limer would then be picked upon. An older male might be asked 'when you alive yet, you could cook?' or about whether any remaining hair is really his. An accident or mistake might be thrown back at the 'guilty' party many times, with appellations such as 'mother-cunt'. Such *picong* almost always remains good-humoured, because the recipient knows that they are being judged by their ability not to *take this on*. This often witty and always barbed invective between friends makes the lime a kind of training ground in which one is steeled against taking in the abuse which can be received in life. There is a version of madness called *tabanca*. This afflicts people not because they have lost a relationship, but because they then discover that they allowed that relationship to get inside them, and when it ended they became distracted and disorientated. One of the most common expressions heard in response to any misfortune, from a passing insult to the break-up of a relationship, is *doh (don't) take it on*. In other words implying don't take it in.

Most Trinidadians would certainly assert humour and wit as central to their self-definition and would see it as contributing to their sense of cool and style. A person without a sense of humour, who can't take insults, is seen as *ignorant* and prone to violence, a label Trinidadians use of their Caribbean rivals, the Jamaicans. This keeping of things on the surface also means the freedom to construct oneself and not be categorized by circumstance. In London when two middle-class people meet they tend to ask each other 'and what do you do?' – meaning their employment. But most Trinidadians consider this highly inappropriate. One works simply because one needs to earn money, so this is entirely the wrong source of self-definition. Asking what work someone does tells you nothing significant about them. It is the things one chooses freely to do that should define you, not the things you have to do. Freedom in self-construction seems central.

It is again at Carnival that one comes to appreciate the further implications of not seeing the essential nature or truth of a person as a property located deep within. One of the main themes of Carnival is the revelation of truth. Carnival starts at night with a festival called *Jouvert* derived from the French *jour d'ouvert* or the opening of the day. People dress as creatures of the night, such as devils, or come out covered in mud (London's Notting Hill has an appealing variant: covering your body in chocolate). Sometimes they carry placards with scandals and accusations. Gradually they move towards the centre of town where they are revealed by the dawn. In 1988, one of the most striking costumes represented a current calypso and was called Bacchanal Woman. A huge figure wore a dress festooned with eyes. Bacchanal is the disorder that follows scandalous revelation. The classic example is where a strict schoolteacher has tried to portray herself as thoroughly respectable, until a pregnancy reveals something else going on. People try constantly not to reveal the truth about themselves but Carnival brings the things of the night into the light of revelation.

The point all this makes about lies is that people are constantly trying to hide them. And where is the obvious place to hide things? Well, deep inside where other people can't see them. So the truth that emerges at Carnival is premised on exactly the opposite set of metaphors as that of our own depth ontology. For Trinidadians it is entirely obvious that truth resides on the surface where other people can easily see it and attest to it, while lies are to be found in the hidden recesses deep within. A person's real being, then, is also on the surface, and evident. The deep person, who keeps things stored close to himself or herself and out of view, is viewed as just dishonest. The point, of course, is that truth is neither intrinsically deep nor on the surface. Neither set of metaphors can be judged as right or wrong. It is simply that there is no reason why any other population should have a concept of superficiality which sees the deep inside as true and significant and the surface as false and insignificant. In many ways the Trinidadians seem to have a rather more obvious logic of spatial metaphors of truth and being than we do.

These differences in metaphors, reflecting differences in the concept of being, may use idioms of time as well as of space. If the self is not deep inside it is also not viewed as constant. We see the self as growing, based on things that are accumulated. So occupation, social status and position create substance which is accumulated within. This comes from a historical preference for relatively fixed identities and hierarchies. In earlier times a person was defined by birth. We now prefer an apparently meritocratic ideal which defines them more by cumulative achievement. But Trinidadians may not be aiming for such a sense of an incremental self, which would be regarded as both false and imposed by position. A person today should not be judged by what they used to be, but what they are now. Instead we have to imagine a situation in which being is constantly re-created through a strategy of display and the response of that moment. In going to a party, or forming a relationship, the individual usually aims high. They attempt the best style, the wittiest verbal agility and, if possible, the most impressive partner. But one only finds out if this is actually who you are from the response of the day; how people react to you and appraise you. It is each particular and assumed transient activity that tells one who one is. It is the event itself that gives judgement. However, this is only a specific event or relationship, so that the position has to be recovered again on the next occasion.

The advantage of a transient self is that it is less subject to institutional construction and judgement. It is not given by formal recognition or occupation. This means that comparatively speaking it is a self that can feel free – which for Trinidadians is tantamount to saying it is more real or truthful. Men and women prefer to judge the state of their relationship by the way they treat each other at that time. They are suspicious of the way an institution, such as marriage, can lead to one side taking the other for granted, and no longer having to make constant the attention that signifies that the relationship remains true. For Trinidadians, marriage as an institution can easily make a relationship false, since one can mistake its formal nature for its reality, which lies in the actual way each treats the other in the present. This is one reason why people prefer to wait for marriage until they are very established in their relationship, often with several children.

There is a problem with the kind of historical determinism which always explains the present by a search for roots, by a narrative of how people got to be as we now find them. Social science tends to be more concerned with how things connect up with each other today. The past has certainly made its contribution. Perhaps the huge emphasis Trinidadians put on freedom, the freedom to construct themselves through style, rather than being defined by occupation, does indeed show an influence from slavery. The past experience of oppression might put a premium on freedom today. But anthropologists prefer to see things in comparative perspective, looking for analogies in other societies. Anthropologists writing about Papua New Guinea, for example, have argued that, there too, people prefer to judge by appearances.[7] Members of a community parade and dance for considerable periods in front of others. By doing so, not only can the observers see how cohesive they are currently as a group, but also the individuals doing the parading see, in the eyes of those judging them, who they actually are. Have they been able to look good as individuals and cohesive as a group? My sense is that populations who are relatively egalitarian prefer metaphors which suggest that people are to be defined by their current abilities and achievements; that they should lose that achieved position when those abilities wane. It follows that they tend to see truth and being as on the surface. By contrast, strongly entrenched societies with long histories of institutionalization, whether of class or position, tend to see being and truth as deep within the self and relatively constant.

In such a context clothes do not just mean something quite different; they are something quite different. In these egalitarian societies, they are the very forms by which one can discover who one actually is. It then makes a great deal of sense to spend rather more time being concerned with how one looks, if how one looks is who one is. Not a reflection of who one is, but actually who one is. Our own notion of being as depth has some surprising consequences. For example, we have this very peculiar ideal about looking natural, which tends to imply that putting on make-up and clothes is false and superficial. But why should we assume this? Why should the fact that one person has freckles tell us who they are? Or that one person is born uglier than another person, and so can portray evil or a debased character on the stage? We see the natural just like the deep as being the truth of a person. The Trinidadian conception, by contrast, is that who we are is not at all given by the happenstance of physiognomy – our face when we wake up in the morning. Why on earth should the natural look of a person be a guide to who that person is? By contrast, a person who spends time, money, taste and attention in creating a look, where the final look is the direct result of all that activity and effort, can properly be discovered in their appearance. Because now one is judging what they have done, not what they happen to look like originally. We are judging them by their labour, not their birth. One aspires by the act of self-cultivation. Other people can then see if you are all that you claim thereby to be, or if actually you are clearly not up to that mark.

Trinidad is a street corner society where such failures are going to be commented upon, often within a few hundred metres of setting out from your house. People love to pronounce in public upon how another person looks. But again, if we push ourselves beyond our usual metaphors, we can see that this can make perfectly good sense. Trinidadians do label people as plumbers or lawyers, rich or poor, or for that matter black or white, but regard this as superficial, compared to a judgement as to how they have constructed themselves, whether they can strut their stuff. My intention is not really to favour one view of being over the other, although it's hard not to see the Trinidadian view as rather clearer and more consistent than our own. The consequence, for present purposes, is that when Trinidadians spend far more attention on clothing, and make it more of a priority in their lives, they are not being deluded or more facile.

This first case study also provides a clear illustration as to what I mean when I claim an ambition to be an extremist. We go to an island in the Caribbean and find that there is a relationship to clothing unlike anything we had imagined. But we achieve this understanding through an extreme particularism. Anthropologists can always become still more parochial if we choose. It is something we do with relish because it proves our scholarship. Only after living there for a year could I start to understand the diversity of Trinidad itself. By then even the general term Trinidadian looked suspect. Because the people I am dealing with are Indo and Afro, big-shot and grass-roots, men and women, elderly and children. Actually they are Jonas and George, Simone and Rhoda. Ethnography is a devotion to the particular, what was special about these individual people at this time. Yet to understand one tiny microcosm of this population – why impoverished women had so many shoes – one needed to interrogate a basic philosophical assumption about what it is to be human. I needed to challenge our fundamental theory of ontology, that is, the philosophy of being, to expose the assumptions we make about where being is located and the multiplicity of metaphors and assumptions that flow in all directions from the presumption that being is deep.

We thereby gain an appreciation that what we had assumed to be a universal was itself a particular. That ontology is a cultural construction and not an inherent truth. But demolishing the foundations of Western philosophy in order to understand impoverished Trinidadian women's relationship to their shoes strikes me as entirely worthwhile. It justifies the struggle to bring the two extremes of universalism and particularism back into conversation with each other. After all, the aim of anthropology is understanding, in the sense of empathy. I suppose I was always trying to imagine what it would be like to be in their shoes.

There is another reason for starting with this particular example. The point made here relates to more than just clothing. The term superficiality and the assumptions we make about where being is located form part of a much larger denigration of material culture in our own society, where materialism itself is viewed as superficial. Becoming a consumer society is generally seen as symptomatic of a loss of depth in the world. This example of a universalizing attitude to modern mass consumption is clearly expressed in another branch of philosophy; the writings on postmodernism, which may be viewed as merely the most recent manifestation of aesthetic and philosophical ideologies which lie at the core of Western thought. Here though we are embarked on a journey that is intended to rescue, not just clothing, but the whole of material culture and the people who study material culture from this same accusation of superficiality. To show why people in places such as tribal Papua New Guinea may be resolutely more materialistic than we are, and may accept with little problem that people are constituted by things and appearances. So demolishing our presumptions about superficiality can only be a start. Next we need to look in more detail at how things, such as clothing, come not to represent people, but to actually constitute who they are. In pursuit of that goal we are now going to shift from Trinidad to India. Once that was hard to imagine. But thanks to Google Earth, just zoom out a little, move the globe a little, and now zoom right back in.

The Sari[8]

A sari is a single piece of entirely unsewn cloth, usually around 6 metres, worn by being draped around the body. Usually these days it is worn in association with a petticoat, a blouse piece, and beneath these, pants and a bra. The aim of this section is not to tell you how Indian women wear a sari, or how the sari represents their identity. Quite the opposite. The intention is to explain how the sari wears the Indian woman, how it makes her what she is – both woman and Indian. If, in Trinidad, clothing challenges what we meant by the concept of *being*, in India we shall see how a phrase such as 'being a woman' is also subject to comparative analysis. As will become apparent, being a woman is quite different if it is accomplished through wearing a sari rather than through wearing a skirt or dress. Clothes are among our most personal possessions. They are the main medium between our sense of our bodies and our sense of the external world. First then let's consider how it feels to wear a sari.

In the now widespread Nivi style, the sari is draped from right to left, passing over the lower body twice – the second time in a cluster of fan-shaped pleats – and the upper body once. The *pallu*, the free and usually more decorated end of the sari, falls over the left shoulder down to the waist. Given the asymmetry of the sari, no sensation in one part of the body is repeated in any other. The right leg does not feel like the mirror of the left. The two shoulders and the two breasts are touched by the garment in quite different ways. The right shoulder can remain untouched by the sari, while the left bears the weight of the pallu. The right breast feels the pressure of the pleats of the pallu pulled across the bosom, whereas the left one feels exposed, covered from the front but visible from the side. The right side of the waist is hot from the pleats passing over it, but the left side is uncovered and cool.

The centre point of the sari – the navel – carries the sensation of being a focal pivot around which the security of the whole garment revolves. Here the pleats are tucked into the drawstring of the petticoat. About a metre of cloth is gathered, with a good 12 cm tucked inside the string, against the belly. This causes perspiration, and a *zari* or starched cotton border may scratch,[9] but these sensations also give reassurance that the pleats are not spilling out. The thighs help define the graceful folds of the pleats that fan out from between the legs. Here again the sensations are asymmetrical. The pleats often lie from right to left in such a way that the first pleat rests on the right leg while the last pleat rests against the left leg. It is how one holds the right leg and knee that defines the shape of the pleats, but it is from the left leg that the sari curves from mid-thigh around towards the back of the body, resting in folds on the back of one's waist to then be brought around from the right side as the pallu. So the curve of a woman's hip and waist is accentuated on the left side. A slight bend at the knee can create a horizontal break in the vertical folds of the sari, giving a woman a more feminine and statuesque look. The ankles always feel slightly crowded as the gathers of the folds of the sari rest against them, their touch made heavier by the 'fall'. When walking, the right leg determines the length of the stride, which is kept in check by the warning tension at the ankle when the stride is too long for the sari. The left leg needs to move a little bit out and forward so as not to trap the pleats between the knees. The pallu may slide off with the movement, in which case the right arm comes up to restore it to the left shoulder, but carefully so as not to crush the cloth. After a few strides the sari may slip down from the left waist, and the left arm needs to pull it back up in order to retain the fan shape of the pleats.

As they sit down, women invariably check that the pallu has not slipped from covering the right breast, and that the waist is not too exposed by the folding of the torso. The folding of the body upon sitting down in a rickshaw or a car tends also to crush the sari in front and threatens the sequence of the pleats. A series of adjustments is required to even out the part of the pallu which is visible in the front; the pleats need to be rearranged to help them retain their order, and the pallu needs to be freed from being trapped beneath the bottom. Different sorts of weather create their own sensations and problems. The perspiration that accumulates where the sari is tucked in or densely bunched is mainly unseen. Indeed, the perspiration running down the legs meets the air circulating there, creating a pleasurable cooling sensation. When the waist becomes too damp and itchy, a woman can push the petticoat string to a fresh patch of skin on the waist. In wet weather the bottom of the sari tends to be soaked first, making it heavy and pulling the whole garment downwards. The sari loses its shape and is harder to control or to feel comfortable in. A wet sari also clings to the body at various points, accentuating curves and dips of its own accord, rather than as intended by the wearer.

Clearly then wearing a sari has a specific feel. But this is only a hint of much more profound differences. To appreciate these we need to zoom in upon just one part of the sari – the *pallu*, the often highly decorated end of the sari that falls over the shoulder. The pallu represents a prosthetic quality to the garment that is not shared by any Western clothing. This is most obvious in its functional usage. As a woman does her household chores, the pallu is in constant use as a kind of third hand, lifting hot vessels in the kitchen, wiping the seat she is about to sit on in a public place, cleaning her spectacles, gathering up rupee notes in a purse-like knot, or protecting her face from smoke and smog. The pallu's presence is so constant and available, so taken for granted, that it almost seems part of the body itself. Yet the same quality that extends the capacity of a person also gives the pallu the power to betray them. When something happens that represents the unwelcome intrusion of the external world upon the self, it may well have the pallu at the end of it. The pallu gets jammed in a car door, flies in your face so that you cannot see, or falls off your head when you are trying to be modest. The same pallu that is used to hold a hot *karhai* (cooking pot) of food may actually catch fire when cooking. Such accidents are all too common, and can result in horrible injury and death. They are not always accidents either. In many instances of *dowry deaths*, the groom's family claim that her pallu caught fire 'accidentally' while she was cooking. On the other hand, desperately unhappy brides typically end their misery by hanging themselves from the ceiling by their pallu.

The close identification between people and the pallu starts with the initial relationship between mother and infant. Most

Indians have their first encounter with the sari before the time
of memory. Mothers use it as a multi-purpose nursing tool.
When breast-feeding they cradle the baby within it, veiling the
operation from the outside world, and use the cloth to wipe the
surplus milk from the baby's lips. The pallu retains this ability
to appear as an extension of the mother, as one woman observed
of her son:[10]

> When he falls asleep he puts my pallu twisted around his thumb
> into his mouth. If I disengage my sari he starts wailing. Sometimes
> people give children pieces of cloth like a hankie or a scarf to get
> them out of the habit of their mothers' pallu. But I never have.
> Several neighbours have suggested it but I think – what is the harm
> if he holds my sari, why give him a separate piece of cloth? He
> plays hide-and-seek with my sari. He keeps hiding behind it and
> showing his face. He keeps doing this until I smile back. He thinks
> I may be angry otherwise. When we sleep next to each other, I
> cover my face and pretend to be asleep. So he moves the pallu away
> to see if I am smiling or laughing. If I don't register any emotion
> he starts crying and keeps calling 'Ma! Ma!' then I have to give
> in and he is happy. And he starts doing the same by covering his
> face and playing the same game himself. He learnt to walk holding
> not my finger, but my pallu.

For the child, the pallu becomes a physical embodiment of their
mother's love, a love they can literally take hold of. The pallu
exemplifies what the psychoanalyst Winnicott has dubbed a 'transitional object'.[11] A child takes time to understand that it is itself
an individual thing, separate from the rest of the external world
as first represented by the mother and her breast. The pallu helps
bridge that awful separation and comforts the child during his
growing awareness of it. A popular version of this idea is the
'comfort blanket' carried by the character Linus in the cartoon
Peanuts. A middle-aged man recalls:[12]

> I had a very good childhood, I think of my mother and my grand-
> mother, you know, showing their love, wiping the sweat off my
> forehead with the pallu, using it like a fan in the summer. My
> mother's mother – I would be lying in her lap with my head in her
> lap and she would just cover my head with the pallu. I would go
> to sleep in this way.

For adults, the ambiguity of the pallu being simultaneously part of someone, yet separate from them, continues when it comes to their own attempts to form relationships. Given the natural propensity of the pallu to slip down from the bosom, the action of constantly covering up one's chest can have the effect, if done well (and some do it *very* well), of constantly drawing attention to the area that is ostensibly being protected. So a man has no idea whether a woman is re-covering herself because of what she does not want him to see, or is pointing out what she *does* want him to see. Another provocative form of manipulation deftly exploits the property of a sari as a draped garment, and consists of swiftly tightening it to accentuate the tautness of the bottom or the smallness of the waist. There is the additional potential for beauty and eroticism in a fabric which may appear transparent when in a single layer but is opaque when worn in several layers. The same subtlety that applies to flirtation is even more commonly applied to the institution of modesty, in which the pallu plays a central role. Most Hindu women have to cover their heads in the presence of certain family members, while most Muslim women have to cover theirs before strangers. Women have considerable scope to manipulate the precise way the pallu is held between the teeth or placed over their head, leaving the observing male quite uncertain as to the attitude that lies behind the action: it might be demure or respectful, tantalizing or truculent. These nuances of modesty and eroticism are used to great effect by those making Bollywood films and television soap operas. Physical contact in public between men and women remains frowned upon. Even married couples promenading in Delhi's parks will not, for example, hold hands. In this context, the pallu becomes an important point of playful contact between grown-up siblings or similarly aged friends. You can tug at it in order to encourage a sister or friend to 'get a move on'. Touching the pallu allows for intimacy in the absence of touching the body itself. If someone gets too attached to another person, they are likely to be teased by having it said that they have 'attached themselves to the other's pallu' (as a television presenter said to a fan who kept phoning her show). On the other hand, and for much the same reasons, in a sexual context touching the pallu can be a very intimate and personal act indeed. In Bengal, for instance, it is traditional for a bride on her wedding night to tie the end of her pallu to her husband's dhoti. These associations also help explain the comment of a sex worker in Kolkata, who reported that she did not like her clients to touch the pallu because she felt it should be reserved for her relationship with her husband.

The full emotional repertoire of the pallu is most clearly seen in watching television melodrama. The scene with the woman applying for a job as a servant has her constantly fiddling with the end of her pallu, betraying her anxiety. The school teacher who thrusts the pallu into her midriff or holds it tight in her fist to ensure that her class knows that she means business. A girl laughing just a bit too hard covers her mouth with the pallu. A woman dabbing with it at her tears thereby also screens her eyes. The pallu is a haven for an embarrassed face and a cover for unseemly emotion. But, as with so many gestures made with the sari, these ambiguities can in turn give rise to an erotic element: often unintentionally, as when covering the mouth suddenly accentuates the eyes, or screening the eyes draws attention to the lips. Thus, while the series, plots and characters may change, the pallu's starring role remains constant.

This intimate relationship between person and cloth is not simply given, by virtue of being born in South Asia. All of this has to be learnt and mastered by each individual. A typical girl in Delhi is not brought up wearing a sari. She will first attempt this intimidating feat at the special 'school farewell' ceremony, which marks the end of the final school year, for girls aged around seventeen. The girls fumble around, scared stiff of the unfamiliar folds, dangerous-looking pins and sudden extrusions of loose cloth. They are continually worried about the risk of slippage, exposure and shame before highly competitive peers, their parents and their teachers. The girls' ability to tame and inhabit this fearsome flood of fabric will be taken as an indicator of their future ability to perform the social roles that will be expected of them. Not surprisingly at this point saris often stay in place thanks largely to discreetly placed safety pins. A girl may then wear the sari a few more times at the weddings of relatives, only to be faced with the occasion in her life when she is most subject to constant scrutiny, her own wedding, where her sari wearing becomes the centrepiece of the performance.

Once married, the neophyte sari wearer strives for social respectability. She must learn to move, drape, sit, fold, pleat and swirl the sari in an appropriate way. She may live in constant fear of embarrassment on moving to her husband's home. She can hardly sleep because she is so afraid that loss of consciousness will lead to her head or knees being uncovered, and as a result she feels stifled in the summer nights. For one woman her worry about the sari falling off leads her to tie her petticoat string so tightly that later on the doctor is convinced she will harm the baby now growing inside her. At the level of safety and practicality, she must try to avoid the frequent injuries that arise from getting the sari caught in doors, machines or, worst of all, the stove.

As an outsider entering a village where all the women wear a sari one just assumes that this has become natural as something obvious and straightforward. But this is not at all the case. One meets women who have worn a sari for forty years and still never feel that they are really in command of the garment. Think of this more on analogy with driving a car. Learning to drive and learning to wear a sari both mark a shift in one's own sense of age; there is a feeling of becoming an adult, with all the new freedoms, capacities, constraints and fears that growing up entails. Both are also public events, and one's competence – or lack of it – are open for others to scrutinize and criticize. Both share the involvement of family, the same pride and fears of the parents, the common assistance of the neighbour, friend or relative who kindly gives the girl extra practice and helps her to hone her skills. Some girls turn out to be 'naturals'. Some, having had the misfortune to fail their test at driving or by tripping over at their school farewell, never achieve real mastery and acquire a new and unwelcome identity as 'poor woman driver/sari wearer' that will burden them for the rest of their lives. Most embark on the new task with difficulty, but through practice over the years gradually come to develop an automatic competence that allows them to proceed without much thought about the mechanics of what they are doing.

Just as in driving a car, for most women, their actions in wearing the sari become increasingly natural and automatic and they lose awareness that they are inhabiting the sari and its requirements. If a woman is lucky and starts to dominate rather than be oppressed by her sari, then eventually such hard-won skills will give her a remarkable flexibility to hide or accentuate those features of her body which she wishes to expose, moderate or cover up completely. Whether she works in a field or an office, she may now have a little money, saved after household expenses have been met, with which to buy her own clothes. If she has the financial resources (many village women never earn enough money to participate fully), she is able to make choices, experiment with colours and materials and she learns to spot a bargain. In other words, she becomes an active consumer of saris. It is during this period that a woman really develops her individual style, making decisions about which colours suit her, which designs she prefers and what kinds of material she is able to best manage and enjoy. This is also the period of her life when she has to juggle the competing demands of children, husband, relatives, neighbours, friends and workplace. These may all constrain her choices, but where she is able, she dresses herself accordingly for these different audiences, occasions and moods.

Just as the sari starts off as far more oppressive than most Western garments, it now has the capacity to be far more powerful. Men working in offices complained that they could not compete with some women, simply because men don't wear a sari. A woman at one with her sari knows exactly how to place her pallu. While everyone else looking at her thinks it is just about to fall from her shoulder, she knows it isn't. She has command of a tool that allows her to express a variety of subtle emotions and claims, manipulating the sari's particular capacity for ambiguity especially with respect to eroticism. The sari by this stage becomes an instrument of power. No one ever achieved such a political mastery of this garment as Indira Gandhi. Somehow her wardrobe represented every region, group and aspiration of hundreds of millions of ordinary Indian women.

To read this account as merely a report on a research project about how Indian women wear a sari would be to miss the key elements being conveyed here. The point of this study is that the sari plays a considerable and generally unacknowledged role in creating a specificity to being an Indian woman that is distinct. The fact that, every day, a person is expected to change her appearance in relation to ever shifting circumstance or encounter makes for a significant difference in how it feels to be a woman. There is a huge contrast with most stitched clothing, which, once put on in the morning, can be largely taken for granted for the rest of the day. Stitched clothing cannot be manipulated in this way and the wearer does not expect to do so. But the sari forces a continued engagement and conversation with its wearer, and a constant pressure to respond to changes in one's surrounding social environment. In the larger book, from which this account is taken, we show how the current struggle between the sari and its main alternative, the *shalwar kamiz*, has become a struggle over what it means to be a modern Indian.

The sari is like a fellow actor, constantly on stage, whose presence must always be remembered. The sari turns a woman into a person who interacts with others and with the self through this constantly shifting material. A sari can be extremely supportive when attended to, helping accomplish all manner of tasks, practical, social and emotional. But when neglected it can be quick to betray, causing others to judge you harshly for quirks of appearance that you did not intend. Such varied and ambivalent experiences with the sari have a far-reaching bearing upon a woman's sense of herself, as an individual. Simply saying that someone is an Indian woman is merely a labelling. By examining the minutiae of sari-wearing we can start to see that there are a multitude of different expectations and experiences that are a direct result of wearing a particular item of clothing. These all create the specific experience of being a sari-wearing Indian woman.

London

The presumption of anthropology lies in such comparative analysis between Trinidad and India. Recognizing that we take for granted our own ways of doing things, and that it is only through coming to appreciate how other people have entirely different experiences and expectations that we can start to challenge our own. That is the intended logic of this chapter. It is only by paying attention to the relationship between people and clothing in Trinidad and in India that a Londoner, such as myself, can in turn find people's relationship to clothes in London extraordinary, exotic and in need of explanation. Why should we think clothing is superficial, why do we wear such static clothing when there are alternatives that are more dynamic? Finally, we become ready to acknowledge why, from other people's perspective, it is we who may be seriously weird.

In its initial conception anthropology tended to treat the places from which anthropologists then came, such as London, as given, relatively unmarked, contrasted with all other places that required explanation. Today we have an anthropology based on a global equality of amazement and exoticism. Just because I was born, brought up in and now live in London doesn't mean that I understand it. Quite the contrary, in some ways as a Londoner I am the least qualified person to engage with London, because it has, for me, this taken for granted quality. In other disciplines, the fashion is to suggest that if we seek to understand the experience of, for example, a transsexual Argentinian shop assistant, we need mainly to give voice to transsexual Argentinian shop assistants. But anthropology has always resisted this kind of politics. Insisting instead that we need an exchange of understanding, where it is the others who can see much more easily the conventions and suppositions upon which we found our daily lives. This implies that we need to treat cosmopolitan sites such as London with the same respect of intense observation and analysis as anywhere else. It is all too easy to sink back into glib generalization when we return to familiar surroundings. Even in Western Europe there are profound distinctions in regional relationships to clothing if we examine them systematically. An example emerged recently in the research of one of my PhD students, Marjorie Murray, who was born and grew up in Chile, but carried out her ethnographic fieldwork in Madrid.

Murray found people's relationships to clothing in Madrid to be completely unlike either her own Chile, or indeed London, where she had come to study for her doctorate. She was struck by the extreme conformity of Madrilenians. When they go out, they wear what they consider to be classic, smart and generally quite expensive clothing, even if they are not wealthy. They spend a considerable amount of time preparing themselves and their appearance before setting forth. It is quite common to use designer labels as part of this ensemble. They also have a huge knowledge of what everyone else is wearing, both people they see on the street and celebrities. By contrast, when they return home, they immediately change into clothing which is generally extremely shabby, often old, even worn or torn. Clothing which makes them look really quite unattractive. In neither the public nor in this private dressing is there much sense of individual expression. Rather, people look to wear what most people will agree is proper and appropriate clothing. Of course this is a huge generalization; no one would have the slightest difficulty in finding endless diversity, subtlety and distinction. But to conduct anthropological enquiry we need to assert comparative generalizations. Murray brings considerable evidence to show that, at least as against London or Chile, Madrid can still be characterized as a place of astonishing convention and conformity. For all our sense of European cosmopolitanism, there are marked particularities to individual cities. Another of my PhD students found that her sister in Italy was so horrified by the kind of grungy appearance that London seemed to have inflicted upon her that she insisted she return to Italy for a kind of sartorial cure.

One reason the people of Madrid may wear still more classic and conservative clothing in public is very likely associated with their history as the capital of Spain, and previously the Spanish Empire. Rather than expressing themselves as individuals, they feel responsible for representing the grandeur of Spain itself, of which they are the centre. They make it very hard for any individual who tries not to conform to the public ideal of respectability. Indeed, wearing shabby clothes at home seems to confirm that the role of clothing is to demonstrate this public appearance and is not a medium for individual or private self-expression.

In London the situation is largely reversed. London is striving today to be a capital of cool partly in refutation of a previous time when it was a capital of Empire – now seen as extremely uncool. To merely conform to a generic public fashion, or to resort to designer labels, is likely to see the wearer branded as sartorially incompetent. Styles that deliberately repudiate respectability are often the vanguard of fashion. In London individuals are exhorted to express themselves, even find themselves, through their clothes. As most women in London will attest, this is a hell of a lot harder than it sounds. It does, however, lead to a very different understanding of what fashion itself is. Most theories of fashion, most studies of fashion, look to the fashion industry, its organization, pressures and patterns to account for fashion.[13] But actually there is good evidence that most people choose their clothing as much despite as because of that fashion industry. If one glances across the range of clothing actually worn on London underground trains or in the street, things look very different from the fashion magazines that those same people are reading.

Currently, I am involved in a large-scale research project on denim,[14] which is what, on any given day, around half the population actually wears. Certainly the fashion industry tries to incorporate denim by developing an expensive array of designer denim. This is the denim the magazines will display and write about. But the vast majority of denim that people actually wear is relatively nondescript. Over the last decade, the rise of cheap supermarket denim has been much more significant than the rise of designer denim. It is cheap denim that one mainly sees on a given street. Since the style barely changes from decade to decade, it is hard to argue that this shows us responding to the pressures of fashion in its restless search for new profitable niches.

So perhaps we need to look elsewhere for a theory of women's fashion in London. Just as in India and Trinidad, we need to take seriously the experience of the women who wear it. The critical moment in that experience may well be when a woman gets up in the morning, examines a full wardrobe and yet feels an overwhelming fear that she has 'absolutely nothing to wear'. Another PhD student, Sophie Woodward, wrote her thesis on this act of getting dressed in the morning.[15] She reasoned that merely to observe what women wear on the street provides only a partial glimpse. Because so often, when they first get dressed, they try on a more adventurous set of clothing, maybe more than one, before losing confidence and returning to their default clothing. I decided never to enquire too deeply as to just how exactly she managed to conduct this fieldwork, but this is precisely what she found. Fashion in London is much more about anxiety than it is about industry. It is this anxiety that may explain the major changes in fashion over the last few decades.

A paper called 'The little black dress is the solution. But what is the problem?' reflected on these changes.[16] Why can every other colour only at best aspire to be the new black? Where and when did this happen? Black may have some association with the chromophobia that seems to have possessed modernism from time to time, but that didn't prevent a veritable explosion of colour in the 1960s, not far short of Austin Powers. Most of what I have written so far concerns women, but I too experienced these changes. I see them rather as those described by Salman Rushdie in his wonderful children's book *Haroun and the Sea of Stories*. The book's premise is that there is some evil mechanism that is taking away the vital stream of stories that course through the veins of our world. During my lifetime I have been witness to a similar dreadful loss. There has been a gradual leaching out of colour and print from the world of clothing in London. Just as in Rushdie's story, it is as though somewhere there is a vast hole through which colour and print is leaking out, leaving an increasingly grey, brown and black world of clothing that makes for a drab, colourless environment, only partially compensated for by a few exceptions such as sportswear and the little red dress.

I feel personally affronted by this assault, since I too suffer from this same affliction. When I started lecturing I was still wearing a bright orange jersey and a necklace of shells retained from my fieldwork in the Solomon Islands. But I was already looking like an anachronistic *hippie*. Of course, being a hippie was itself merely conventional to that time, and I have shifted with all the subsequent movements towards the colourless. Today I seem to have ended up with conventional male brown, indigo and black, with classic Armani-emulating cuts for more formal wear, and jeans for the more informal. About the most exciting possibility left for me to discover is a new shade of grey.

To explain all this we need to both examine and then account for the underlying problem. My own investigation came from a year spent shopping with people from one street in North London.[17] I found that women's anxieties about clothes come in all shapes and sizes. Sharon, for example, is reaching her fortieth birthday and sees this as a watershed in terms of consolidating her appearance and her wardrobe. For she is 'fed-up with getting it all wrong'. A full-time mother of three children living in state housing, she contrasts herself with a close friend who, she comments, 'could wear a piece of rag and look gorgeous'. Recent fashion disasters included being the only person to wear evening dress at a party for her mother-in-law, because she had believed her mother-in-law's claim that everyone else would dress up. Also driving 15 miles across London with her family to a christening, and then turning back since she simply had to replace the blue cotton summer dress she was wearing with another one that had less of a 'T-shirt' style neckline.

Sharon's anxieties could be labelled as mid-life. But the situation is not much different shopping with Charmaigne, a highly fashionable eighteen-year-old who is extremely self-conscious of her 'ideal' figure (she dances in videos for vanguard pop music), and excels in choosing items which she considers most appropriately draw attention to her body. But feeling she needs to look a little more grown up, she decides she needs a floral print dress. During the course of our expedition to Brent Cross shopping centre, we encounter hundreds of possible floral prints. The issue of cost is not raised, only of suitability. There is certainly no lack of choice. The problem for Charmaigne, again and again, was knowing whether she actually liked a print or not and therefore being able to determine what her taste was or could be. In the end she returns home empty-handed. Charmaigne certainly does not lack knowledge of clothes: her problem is knowing what her own taste in clothes might be with respect to an unfamiliar genre. One can have a fine sense of the nuances of language without knowing what one wants to say.

This is why in England there is such an appeal to those who can provide clear direction. To watch a programme called *What not to Wear* and pray there are some simple rules one can follow. Or, at a greater extreme, sign up to a company such as *Colour Me Beautiful* which claims a whole science of clothing that will tell you exactly what colour is right for you. So it is possible to document and characterize this anxiety at the core of fashion, but we also need to account for it. Why has it grown over the last few decades so that people feel unable to wear much of what is easily available in the shops? Here anthropology can step in with its comparative perspective. What makes the situation in London so different from the previous examples?

In India, women who wear a sari are subject to a very well established set of rules and social conventions. A woman who wears something inappropriate will soon be made well aware of her *faux pas*. By comparison, clothing in London is much less guided by order and social convention. It has become quite extraordinarily diverse and subject to rapid changes. So both the constraint, but also the support, of social convention have diminished. Advice from the fashion industry is much harder to use. Once there was some consistency and one was confident in how long skirts should be worn that year. Hemlines around the country went up and down in unison. Now advice is as voluminous as it is contradictory, and despite reading multiple magazines, most people are not too sure what fashion actually is at any point of time. This is despite some brilliant fashion 'agony aunts' (my own heroine being Hadley Freeman of *The Guardian*). But then people are much more suspicious of commercial statements about the current norms of fashion. Perhaps more importantly much of this disengagement from fashion comes from the overwhelming pressure to express the individual and not merely follow fashion whatever it may be. This leads to a suspicion in London of genres such as designer brands which for adults may be seen as vulgar or stupid. Entirely different from the situation in Madrid.

If in London people bear individual responsibility for developing their own sense of style, this makes London seem much more like Trinidad. But there are separate issues which make London very different from Trinidad. People in London are relatively circumspect in expressing their opinions about how others look. Strangers would never shout out comments on the street to a passing woman, in the way they seem to do in Trinidad every few minutes. Comments in London are rarely direct; they are more often based on banter, or irony or said to a third person, rather than directly to the individual in question. As a result, individuals in London find it much more difficult to gain a purchase on this external presentation of themselves. They simply feel unsure about what other people think about them, and then in turn they become increasingly insecure that they even know what they think about themselves. At least with overt criticism you know where you stand. In London this is replaced with paranoia about what people might be saying behind your back – from where they can get a clear view that one's bottom really is too big. It is perhaps no surprise that the key television programme was called not *What to Wear* but *What not to Wear*.

Without the social norms of India and the explicit critical comments of Trinidad, women feel a lack of support in developing their own personal preference. The expression 'I may not know about art but I know what I like' is replaced by the opposite feeling that they do know a great deal about clothing but are not at all sure what they like. In some ways the nail in the coffin of certitude and confidence has been feminism. While there have been some retreats and disavowals in recent years, there have clearly been greater advances in the effective impact of feminism in London as compared to India or Trinidad. Feminism is devoted to the empowerment of women to make choices for themselves and not be dictated to by external pressures. This is entirely positive in terms of equality. But it places still more of a burden on individuals to know for themselves what it is they want and who they want to be. And in the modern world that is becoming one of the hardest of tasks. All of this culminates in a situation where the heart of fashion becomes anxiety. So for London, paradoxically, freedom ends up as a conformity that can be quite drab, but a conformity that is entirely different in cause and effect from that of Madrid.

Academics take delight in repudiating what has been called the 'intuitively obvious'. We gain far more credit if our insights appear original and challenging. But that doesn't in itself make them wrong. The situation is full of ironic contradictions: freedoms that create anxiety, empowerment that feels oppressive, individualism that leads to conformity. Let's be clear as to the implications of this argument. On a political front the much larger and more significant problem with feminism is surely that it has not been successful enough, as yet. I am a student of the 1970s and 1980s, with the same commitments. I am extremely frustrated by the backtracking on what I took as irreversible progress towards equality. But that doesn't stop us appreciating feminism's contradictions – its contribution to this huge burden of freedom. I would hardly advocate a return to authoritarian sartorial codes and unwarranted respect for the voice of industry elites. An anxiety when shopping and dressing, or the feeling that a full wardrobe appears to have 'nothing in it', may, on reflection, be a price worth paying.

Conclusion: A Good Fit?

The intention here is merely to make sense of what, on reflection, is a relationship to clothes that now seems a good deal more peculiar in London than in India or Trinidad. London achieves a spectacular sense of drabness in the teeth of an abundant selection of colourful alternatives hanging in at least some shops, if only we would choose to buy them. What all this demonstrates is the vast range of possible relationships between the concept of the self, the person and clothing. There is nothing new in this. If we look at the longer term it becomes still clearer that it isn't just the clothing that is changing, it's the other side of the equation, the self, that is changing. Mostly this book summarizes my own work here, and that of my students, but no apology is required for a quick excursion to visit a brilliant account of this historical trajectory – *The Fall of Public Man* by Richard Sennett.[18]

Concentrating on material from France, Sennett reflects on the period before the French Revolution; what is sometimes called the *ancien régime*. At this time people were largely expected to dress according to their station in life. People assumed that they would know from clothing who a person was: a butcher, servant, prostitute or gentlewoman. As in many parts of the world, at different times there might be sumptuary laws; making any attempt to dress above one's station in life was illegal. It was only right to make fun, in public, of a person dressing in a manner inappropriate to their occupation. So clothing at that time did not represent some authentic inner person. Rather, people were expected to live up to the conventional category that their clothing represented. Sennett traces various changes in this fundamental relationship. One is the rise of theatre and the idea of acting. One consequence of being conscious that people may be acting a part is the idea that a person who is not acting is being natural. A corollary is that people perhaps ought to be natural when not explicitly acting.

Then the whole relationship between nature, the self and appearance is thrown into confusion by the French Revolution. This creates a slew of new ideals about truth and the person. At one time there was a cult of almost nakedness to express the ideal that the real self should not be hidden by artifice, which now includes clothing itself. From here we can see the start of the liberal trajectory that emphasizes the self itself as a goal in life. This leads eventually to the post-1960s Californian ideal of spending one's life looking for the true, natural, authentic self. So most people today, in places such as England or the US, come to believe that getting clothes right is part of an appropriate exploration of who one really is. Clothes don't so much change us as reveal us, even to ourselves: reveal the true inner and relatively constant self within. Typically we look for something in the shops that is original but not too showy, modest but not stuffy because – well, that's really what we are like, isn't it?

This brief discussion of Sennett's work has brought us full circle, back to the idea of authentic inner selves and the intrinsic superficiality of clothing; a philosophical supposition whose assumed universality was repudiated by the example of Trinidad. Hopefully there is a cumulative conclusion to these three case studies that supports the introduction to this chapter. In three very different instances it becomes clear that we cannot regard clothing as a form of representation, a semiotic sign or symbol of the person. It is this form of analysis, not the clothing, that may now appear to us as superficial. Instead we have discovered something really quite profound. That the concept of the person, the sense of the self, the experience of being an individual, are radically different at different times and in different places, partly in relation to differences in clothing. In each case we have found that clothing plays a considerable and active part in constituting the particular experience of the self, in determining what the self is.

In Trinidad people use clothes to find out who they are at that particular moment of time. In India the experience of being a woman is different, when one is expected to constantly shift appearance in relation to each shift in circumstance. In Madrid clothing helped to retain the cosmological ideal of Madrid as a centre of civilization. While in London clothing was found to be a source of anxiety, precisely because of the increasing pressure on individuals to express themselves, combined with the growing difficulty in determining one's own individual taste. So notwithstanding our increasingly common expectations of education and lifestyle, the supposed homogenizing effects of global capitalism, we have found striking regional differences in our relationship to clothing. This in turn has shown us that there remains also considerable diversity in who and what we think we are. That is not something that strikes me as superficial at all. So even if the same retail clothing chains are now to be found from São Paulo to Seoul this doesn't mean that the experience of wearing that clothing has been reduced to a single expressive form. One further conclusion is that the role of anthropology, committed to learning from comparative studies of humanity, is by no means diminished by global capitalism and modernity. In some ways the fun is only just beginning.

This chapter has also tried to exemplify the argument, introduced in the prologue, that anthropological studies of material culture should strive for a vision of extremism. But in this quest we still have a long way to go. The bulk of this chapter was devoted to an immersion in the rich lather of ethnography, luxuriating in the detail: the sensuality of touch, colour and flow. A study of clothing should not be *cold*; it has to invoke the tactile, emotional, intimate world of feelings. The first task of the anthropologist is to convey these feelings empathetically: what it feels like to wear a sari, where it presses on the body, and where you sweat. How you flirt and how to keep modest. How awful it is to be the only person dressing up for the party. How we can shop for hours and hours and not be able to buy any one of a thousand alternatives on offer. We have immersed ourselves in the minutiae of the intimate.

The next chapter moves us upwards to much more austere and colder climes. Up to the extremes of generalization, abstraction and philosophy, to ask if it is possible to have a theory of material culture and whether we can reach general conclusions about the nature of both humanity and our essential materiality. But even if we reach that peak, we don't want to be stuck there. The aim is not at all to become a philosopher. The aim of anthropology is to take any such pure, clean philosophy and drag it back down to the valley, to the muddy terrain of particularity and diversity. Much of this chapter has been concerned, not with clothing as material culture, but with clothing as clothing – with issues about wearing and texture that are highly specific to clothing and which will contrast with later chapters that concentrate on other genres such as housing or media. But clothing has achieved one task especially well. It has shown us how, in the hybrid world of everyday life, it is often these intimate and sensual realms that are most effective in determining the acceptability and plausibility of the regimes of thought that we call rationality or even ontology. Through the realm of clothing, we can see how, for most peoples, systems of thinking about the world also have to *feel* right.

2

Theories of Things

From Hedonism to Functionalism

The intention of this chapter is to argue for a theory that can explain the findings of the last. Already we are withdrawing from a comfortable idea that we start with people who make things which represent them or others. It is now clear that in material culture we are concerned at least as much with how things make people as the other way around. But that was the last chapter. By the end of this chapter the very conception of things as opposed to persons will come into question; rather, we will end up with processes that give us the illusion that these are discrete entities that make each other. This chapter is not intended to present *the* or *the only* such theory. Many of my colleagues in my own department and in other universities have complementary approaches to that taken here. Some give more emphasis, for example, to the properties of materials such as wood and stone, rather than of artefacts, or take a different route through phenomenology. But at least this chapter will hopefully demonstrate that it is possible to create plausible and helpful theories of *stuff*.

This demonstration will start in the form of a personal story, or search. Beginning with my earliest attempts at such a theory, it will then move upwards to the core theory of objectification as derived from the philosopher Hegel and as then transformed by later writers such as Marx and Simmel. Then we will detour to consider the nature of materiality itself. The chapter will conclude with a consideration of the wider consequence of these theories. Much of this is going to be hard work, even in the rather vulgarized versions of philosophy employed here. If you really can't bear such cold abstractions, you may even decide to skip forward a chapter. But don't despair. In the subsequent chapters we can hopefully once again get down and dirty.

My initial training was as a student in anthropology and archaeology but with an emphasis upon the latter, which to be honest seemed the more romantic of the two. I worked on several archaeological excavations; the very first of them was a Roman pottery factory in the surprisingly suburban environs of Muswell Hill, London. Later more exotic ventures included participation in an attempt to discover the lost empire of Srivijaya in the jungles of Sumatra. Seeing tigers in the wild, excavating in massive caves, watching the morning mists lift from valleys of rice terracing, being taught to swear in Indonesian by local maidens, holidaying in Bali. Life could have been worse. The fact that we conspicuously failed to find the lost empire of Srivijaya merely seemed a generous gift of future opportunities to others. I then attended lectures in London on ancient China, wrote papers in Cambridge about the Indus Civilization of South Asia and, with a fellow student, called ourselves an expedition and studied pottery-making in the Ambon region of Eastern Indonesia.

After graduating, I was employed for two years as government archaeologist by the national museum of the Solomon Islands in the South Pacific through a voluntary scheme,[1] one moment viewing tribal menstrual huts with the anthropologist Roger Keesing, who had written my student textbook,[2] then collecting recipes for cooking children from people who had, in times gone by, eaten them (I will spare you the details, though it involved slaughtering young pigs of the opposite sex, and earth oven pits). Mostly trying to document and protect evidence for the past, partly through new legislation. Trekking barefoot with machetes through forests to discover abandoned hill forts. Then relaxing with fellow volunteers by snorkelling over coral, while lazily passing half empty flagons of Australian wine back and forth over the still surface of the reef-enclosed sea. Two more difficult years.

Some stubborn streak of tedious academic concern somehow seemed to survive all this. The Ambon expedition had already focused upon pottery manufacture.[3] It explored the way social and cultural differences, such as that between Muslim and Christian potters, were represented, not by different pots, which were identical, but through distinctions in the ways these same pots were manufactured. This interest in pottery derived from my point of transition between working as archaeologist and anthropologist. My start with that excavation in Muswell Hill made it clear why archaeologists have a special concern with pottery. Many ancient sites are strewn with pottery fragments, and sometimes not a whole lot else. So the route to the reconstruction of ancient times is usually rather too dependent upon the ways these pottery fragments were interpreted. The temptation was to surrender oneself to their extensive presence. So one would read, in those days, of prehistoric Europe being invaded by the Impressed Beaker People (on reflection they must have looked pretty odd). It seemed sensible to reconsider such simplistic identifications through analogy with contemporary populations and the significance (or insignificance) of pottery in their lives, such as could be observed by ethnographic study.

Later, my return to Cambridge as a graduate student led to me re-locating to a village in north-west India where I was to live for a year in order to collect data for my PhD. The problem I set myself sounded quite simple. The potters in this village produced a range of over fifty pottery shapes, each with their own name and function. As such they were analogous with the assemblages of pottery that were the source of so much archaeological interpretation. Given the additional information available when working in a living society, I asked what precisely explained this particular range of pots. The book that resulted was called *Artefacts as Categories*,[4] and was partly inspired by ideas at the time concerned with categorization processes. One of the book's arguments, however, bears repetition, since it dealt directly with perhaps the most protracted argument to be found in the study of material culture, which is the role of the term *function*. Function tends to remain our default gear in driving towards any explanation of why we have what we have. It is the way we label goods from frying pans to swimwear. But as well as dominating colloquial relationships to things it also provides a powerful trajectory of academic thinking. The adage 'form follows function' was prominent in modernism and remains a trope in design and architecture.

Just when it seemed to have pretty much died out, the idea of function has recently made a rather spectacular comeback with a key role in the many explanatory models, based on evolution, that are becoming prevalent in both archaeology and anthropology. These models almost always depend upon function, as an aspect of humanity's adaptation to its environment. The analogy is with Darwin's Galapagos finches, each developing itself as a living tool to exploit some niche that ensured its survival. There is a huge current fashion for evolutionary style explanations of more or less any and every aspect of human behaviour. You will find such research constantly reported in respected journals such as *The Economist* and on television. It is well represented in my own department. Today this kind of evolutionary anthropology may well be more influential than social anthropology. To be honest I find it impossible to take much of it seriously. I become quite offended when some pundit for this approach appears on television under the title of anthropologist and explains in a deadpan voice why changes in the divorce rates over the last fifty years can be understood by factors connected with humanity's original descent from the trees.

The objection is really quite simple. If our social and cultural customs were indeed, in any way, connected to such functions, then that would have produced a relatively homogeneous humanity whose variation correlated largely with differences in its environment. But social anthropology exists because humanity developed quite otherwise. In one small area, such as Papua New Guinea, almost any generalization one might wish to make about human behaviour can be refuted. There are tribes who privilege homosexuality, eat their ancestors or their enemies, make men menstruate (by bleeding their penises), dance interminably, categorize their natural world systematically, fight constantly, decorate gaudily, develop brilliantly esoteric cosmological ideals about almost any philosophical supposition one could name. But each of these communities believes its customs to be entirely natural and proper, and assumes it is others who are bizarre and mistaken. The Solomon Islanders from whom I collected those recipes saw the killing and eating of a child as simply a necessary means

of gaining a source of power (*mana*) for the tasks they undertook.
In other words they saw this as a moral act rather than the reverse.
Quite apart from the exotic distinctions represented by Melanesia,
we are all more familiar with cultural differences between, say,
the peoples of Japan and Amazonia, France and Sri Lanka,
Kensington and King's Cross. I simply cannot see any correlation
or even much effect on the environment. The climate remains
fairly constant across London suburbs. Accounts that claim
otherwise are hugely popular, but perhaps because their apparent
explanations make life seem so much simpler.

When a colleague informs me that, for a society in Africa with
high infant mortality, grandparenting turns out to be critical to
family reproduction I respect this as serious science. But only
when it relates to a group that is struggling to reproduce, to
behaviour that directly bears on that problem. To accept evolutionary effects on any other human behaviour would be to imply
that we adjudicate one society as better adapted in evolutionary
terms than another. But it is not the case that in New Guinea, or
in the UK, one kinship system, ritual, housing type, propensity to
warfare, or anything else is better able to secure social or cultural
reproduction than any other, because of some environmental
factor. Our behaviour is not a matter of adaptation. So the only
thing evolutionary anthropology can tell us about, with any plausibility, is that which we all have and do in common as humanity.
That is a perfectly respectable academic task. But this evolutionary explanation will never tell us much that is relevant to social
anthropology, which focuses on the opposite problem of what we
don't have in common. Evolution isn't going to help us much with
understanding the diversity of stuff either. After all, in the twenty-
first century the environmentalists are hardly celebrating humanity's increasingly adaptive technology, are they?

Let's take a narrower focus, on the very word function. The
problems with this concept should be evident from the last chapter.
In Trinidad, India and London everyone uses clothes to keep
warm and dry, but that tells you pretty much nothing of interest
about our relationship to clothing. I suppose we could argue
whether a sari was more or less functional than a skirt, but very
quickly we would find that we were talking about function in a
very loose fashion. If a sari is better in expressing modesty, is that
a function? If a skirt signals gender distinction, is that a function?

If most of the women in India who mend roads and work in the fields wear saris, does this imply they are more functional than skirts or trousers? As part of my research on Indian village pottery, one of the tasks I set myself was to investigate systematically the explanatory value of the word function in accounting for the shapes I encountered.[5] I had seen such earthenware village pots exhibited in museums, accompanied by catalogues that waxed lyrical about how such traditional artefacts have evolved in perfect harmony with the needs of the villagers and their environment to produce the forms we now encounter. This is usually meant as a snide comment on our own industrial world, which is seen as shops full of superfluous nonsense that we should all regret.

I therefore dutifully observed, for over a year, how water was taken from water pots, food was cooked in cooking pots and such like. Marking the precise position of fingers, forms of pouring and so forth. My conclusion was that while, not surprisingly, people did manage to store water and to cook, the precise shapes of the pots were quite remarkably ill-adapted to the purposes that they were expected to perform. People used large round water pots with narrow mouths, where the water is extracted using a vessel with a long handle. These are quite ineffective. It is impossible to get water out when they are still half-full. The oil lamps tended to go out, sometimes in a very short time, as the wicks sank into the oil. In any case, just as with the previous reflections on clothing, once we observe that they employed eleven different vessels all for exactly the same function of storing water, these differences obviously cannot be accounted for by function.

Actually there never was a functional society, and tribal or village peoples are probably rather less concerned with function per se than office workers or bankers.[6] Yes, they want their boats to keep afloat, but so, when on holiday, do office workers. Trobriand Islanders do not grow massively long yams because they are easier to grow, or to eat. Instead we have to turn to quite other perspectives if we want to know why pots in an Indian village have their precise shape and range. First, the diversity of such pots is hardly random. Most of the fifty shapes observed were made to look different by exploiting just two or three dimensions of distinction. Just as my jackets focus on differences in, say, the number of buttons and shape of the lapel, so these pots vary according to the angle of the rim, how round they are or whether they have a flat base. In turn these differences can be systematically related to their symbolic significance. So, for example, if one thinks of foodstuffs in accordance with Hindu cosmology as a spectrum from the most pure to most impure, then the sequence of cooking pots makes sense. The most open-mouthed with the most angled rims are associated with the most polluting foodstuffs such as meat and beyond that pots for urination for the elderly, while the most closed and rounded forms are associated with milk, which in Hinduism has sacred connotations. A small distinction may mark the version of a pot intended for the festival of Divali, just as Christians might have a Christmas or Easter mug signified by special decoration. Pots that are given through formalized distributions, at certain times of the year, look systematically different from those that can be purchased for money at the market. In short, the reason why fifty different pots are produced reflects the complexity and elaboration of symbolic ritual and social distinctions. If you are still desperate to call these symbolic distinctions a *function* of the pots – well, no one can stop you.

The word culture tells us that societies elaborate what they are and what they do in many different ways. Through kinship, ritual and also through objects. But if we left our findings at this level we would merely return to our basic theory of representation, that of semiotics. The distinction in pots may not be reducible to function, but the last paragraph gives the impression that differences just represent distinctions in, for example, purity against pollution or festivals against secular times. In mainstream social anthropology the tendency was to reduce these symbolic representations, in turn, to some kind of fundamental social distinction. This follows the strictures of the foundational ancestors in the study of social science such as Durkheim. Following in this tradition came Mary Douglas, one of the most eloquent exponents of the study of categories and categorization. When studying, for example, food symbolism she always tried to relate these to prior social distinctions.[7] This issue will be discussed in more detail shortly. A theory of representation, however, tells us little about the actual relationship between persons and things; it tends always to reduce the latter to the former. So this suggested the need for a further ambition: whether it was possible to develop a theory of things per se that did not reduce to social relations.

The first step was to produce a material culture theory that could apply to these pots. I employed two sources in embarking upon this quest. The first was the book *Frame Analysis*,[8] in which the sociologist Goffman argued that much of our behaviour is cued by expectations, determined by the frames which constitute the context of action. We don't charge up on stage to rescue an actress playing Desdemona when she is in apparent distress. There are many elements of theatre which proclaim this as 'enacted' as against *real* violence. People occupy social roles, as fathers or as working in advertising. But then they also play around with such roles. We have to decide whether they are being ironic, or wanting to be taken 'at face value'. They distance themselves from their role in advertising in order to assert that *really* they are artists but just can't yet make a living that way. The important point to extract from this is that the cues that tell us how to interpret behaviour are usually unconscious. They may be in the place where the action is set, or the clothes being worn. When a lecturer suddenly starts a private conversation with a student in the middle of a lecture (I do this once a year to make this point), everyone suddenly becomes acutely aware of the underlying norms of the lecture as a genre. It is a framed activity that determines what is or is not appropriate behaviour. But mostly we remain unaware of this framing that constrains us.

The second source was *The Sense of Order* by the art historian Gombrich.[9] Unlike all his other books, this focused, not upon the art work, but the frame in which the art work was set. Gombrich argued that when a frame is appropriate we simply don't see it, because it seamlessly conveys to us the mode by which we should encounter that which it frames. It is mainly when it is inappropriate (imagine a Titian framed in perspex, a Hirst in baroque gilt) that we are suddenly aware that there is indeed a frame. A more radical version of Gombrich's thesis could argue that art itself exists only in as much as frames, such as art galleries or the category of *art* itself, ensure that we pay particular respect, or pay particular money, for that which is contained within such frames. It is then perhaps the frame, rather than any quality independently manifested by the art work, that elicits the special response we give it as art. With respect to some contemporary art that conclusion seems to me pretty obvious.

These ideas of Goffman and Gombrich could be used to explain my experience of fieldwork. My problem was the degree to which the Indian villagers I lived with thought I was completely bonkers to be spending so much time looking at pottery. What they tried to tell me, again and again, was that – I guess 'lost the plot' would be a fair translation. Sure, the pots were all over the place, but they were a mere backdrop to the action. Sometimes this was literally the case. A village wedding has, as its most important ceremony, a moment where the bride and groom circumambulate a flame in a square space constituted by four towers of pots. These have become sufficiently iconic that a card just showing this tower of pottery works as an unambiguous wedding invitation. As such they exemplify this theory of frames. As the villagers were telling me, the pots are not the point, they are the frame. Material objects are a setting. They make us aware of what is appropriate and inappropriate. They tell us that this is a wedding, that an impure activity. But they work most effectively when we don't actually look at them, we just accept them. To start a discussion about the frame of a painting rather than the painting, the conventions of theatre rather than the play, the pots at a wedding rather than the marriage, the wallpaper of a room rather than the cosy chat we can have together in the room. It's all rather embarrassing; something that should be left unspoken has been inappropriately foregrounded. So between them, these ideas of Goffman and Gombrich constituted an argument for what I called *the humility of things*.[10] The surprising conclusion is that objects are important, not because they are evident and physically constrain or enable, but quite the opposite. It is often precisely because we do not *see* them. The less we are aware of them, the more powerfully they can determine our expectations, by setting the scene and ensuring appropriate behaviour, without being open to challenge. They determine what takes place to the extent that we are unconscious of their capacity to do so.

So my first theory of things starts with exactly the opposite property of stuff than that we would expect. It is not that things are tangible stuff that we can stub our toe against. It is not that they are firm, clear foundations that are opposed to the fluffiness of the images of the mind or abstract ideas. They work by being invisible and unremarked upon, a state they usually achieve by being familiar and taken for granted. Such a perspective seems properly described as *material culture* since it implies that much of what makes us what we are exists, not through our consciousness or body, but as an exterior environment that habituates and prompts us.

This somewhat unexpected capacity of objects to fade out of focus and remain peripheral to our vision, and yet determinant of our behaviour and identity, had another important result. It helped explain why so many anthropologists looked down upon material culture studies as somehow either trivial or missing the point. The objects had managed to obscure their role and appear inconsequential. At a time when material culture studies had an extremely low status within the discipline, and we were seen by most anthropologists as rather pathetic, it seemed that objects had been very successful in achieving this humility, at least within anthropology. There is a wonderfully felicitous phrase, the 'blindingly obvious'. This implies that when something is sufficiently evident it can reach a point at which we are blinded to its presence, rather than reminded of its presence. One of the problems we have in persuading people that the study of blue denim is so significant is that its ubiquity seems to make people regard it as less of interest, rather than more of interest.

If my own contribution to the study of material culture rests on the precedent of one particular anthropologist, then it would certainly be that of Pierre Bourdieu. I believe that one of the premier publications within anthropology remains his book *Outline of a Theory of Practice*. To appreciate the contribution of Bourdieu we have first to track back a bit to the work of another consummate anthropologist, Claude Lévi-Strauss, who more or less invented the tradition that became known as structuralism. I am writing this text two weeks after celebrating his 100th birthday and acknowledging that no other anthropologist so entirely changed the way the world understands itself.

The central idea in structuralism was that we should not regard entities in isolation: a desk, a table, a dining table, a kitchen table. Rather we should start from the relationship between such things. What we are prepared to accept as a dining table depends in large part on the point at which, if it became any smaller, it would appear to be a kitchen table. Both the objects, and the words we use for them, achieve definition by contrast with what they are not, as much as from what they are. As such, structuralism focused on the relationship between things rather than the things themselves. We have just seen this with my Indian pots. A single pot is meaningless. As an example of culture they are an elaboration of shape along systematic dimensions of difference, so we can only understand each in relation to the whole system. Louis Dumont had argued much the same for Indian society itself.[11] One couldn't comprehend people as simply belonging to a caste, that is, a group of people who are endogamous, marrying only amongst themselves, and usually associated with a particular position in Indian society and often also an occupation. That individual caste was part of a caste system, and behind that were the principles or relationships that generated that system. In the case of caste, the principle of hierarchy combined with a structure, such that each element makes sense only in relation to the whole. A caste was defined in part by the other castes that were higher or lower. For Lévi-Strauss, cosmologies and philosophies were representations of such systems of distinctions and dualisms that gave people the ability to see the world as meaningful.

Lévi-Strauss used tribal myths as the paramount exemplification of his structuralism, but sometimes also objects. In a book called *The Way of the Masks*,[12] he suggested that the masks of one tribe of the North West American coast could be a systematic inversion of another mask of the neighbouring tribe. Where the mask of the first tribe has a protuberance, the mask of its neighbours has a depression, and so forth. Up to then we thought we studied a society but, if there are patterns that play games passing from one society to another, suddenly even the term society was no longer an entity to be studied in isolation. Generally, though, for Lévi-Strauss this structuralism was an intellectual activity. What Bourdieu achieves is a demonstration of how these ideas can be used to create a much more satisfactory theory of how people come to be as they are and see the world in the particular way they do – that is, a theory of socialization. How does an individual grow up as a typical Parisian or Thai or Yanomami? In Bourdieu's account the key operator in making us characteristic of our own society is stuff. Most of his examples came from a North African Berber community called the Kabyle. He argues that what, in industrial societies, we now tend to inculcate through formal education happens to children born into Kabyle society through a process of habituation with the order of the things around them. Born in London, I learnt to eat with a knife and fork rather than chopsticks, to sit on chairs rather than squat, to pick my nose in private rather than in public, to fantasize about removing a woman's bra rather than her tunic, because these were the stuff that made up my environment.

Bourdieu, though, following Lévi-Strauss, argued that these things were not to be seen as unconnected entities. Rather, amongst the Kabyle, a child soon came to take for granted the systematic nature of the order of the home interior. One side was dark because another was light. It was high because another was low. This had to be placed on the right side, that on the left. Furthermore, a child would also soon appreciate that the same underlying order of things, discerned in the home interior, was also underlying the order of agricultural implements, or, for that matter, the order of kinship and marriage expectations. High against low, right against left, could apply as analogous in many different domains. A particular society elaborates its cultural practices through an underlying pattern which is manifested in a multitude of diverse forms. By learning to interact with a whole slew of different material cultures, an individual grows up assuming the norms that we call culture. The child doesn't learn these things as a passive set of categories, but through everyday routines that lead to consistent interaction with things, thereby providing for Bourdieu what he termed a theory of practice.

This seems to correspond very well to what I called the humility of things. Objects don't shout at you like teachers, or throw chalk at you as mine did, but they help you gently to learn how to act appropriately. This theory also gives shape and form to the idea that objects make people. Before we can make things, we are ourselves grown up and matured in the light of things that come down to us from the previous generations. We walk around the rice terraces or road systems, the housing and gardens that are effectively ancestral. These unconsciously direct our footsteps, and are the landscapes of our imagination, as well as the cultural environment to which we adapt. Bourdieu called the underlying unconscious order our *habitus*. There is nature, but culture gives us our second-nature, that which we habitually do without thought. Things, not, mind you, individual things, but the whole system of things, with their internal order, make us the people we are. And they are exemplary in their humility, never really drawing attention to what we owe them. They just get on with the job. But the lesson of material culture is that the more we fail to notice them, the more powerful and determinant of us they turn out to be. This provides a theory of material culture that gives stuff far far more significance than might have been expected. Culture comes above all from stuff. But, as often, when on a journey, to climb to the top of one hill then reveals an even higher peak ahead. So let's keep on climbing.

Objectification

Even if one has no intention of becoming a philosopher, many academics would still have an intellectual curiosity about trying to comprehend what all this might mean in more abstract terms. Philosophizing as a process may be seen as a series of steps upwards in abstraction. We start with the need for a theory of stuff as material culture. It seems then reasonable to see material culture as a subset of culture, as indicated in the last section. But then what is culture a subset of? What is the ultimate relationship between the orders of the external world and the constitution of persons? Can we reach a level of understanding which even dissolves away this distinction? At this level we want a philosophical theory that can account for every kind of stuff: bodies, streaming videos, a dream, a city, a sensation, a derivative, an ideology, a landscape, a decay, a philosophy. A theory of everything. If Bourdieu was my inspiration within anthropology, then in turning to philosophy I have an equally clear debt to Hegel. But if Bourdieu is a hard read, then Hegel is excruciating. So in treating with Hegel I am going to turn even more vulgar and academically sinful.

The system of thought Hegel developed is most fully elaborated in a book first published in 1807. This is sometimes translated as the *Phenomenology of the Spirit*, or the *Phenomenology of Mind*.[13] The inconsistency of this translation is instructive. Because the thing the book is about changes during the course of the book, sometimes seeming more like mind and sometimes more like spirit. The *Phenomenology* is at one level a story, based on *Bildung*, or the stories about a hero's progress, popular in Germany at the time. Now the next few sentences are going to sound weird but, as they say, bear with me. The book starts, as good stories should, at the very beginning. Let's imagine something that can stand for a primitive condition without consciousness. An amoeba, perhaps. But this particular amoeba does have one thing going for it. A drive to have consciousness of something other than itself. So it posits the idea of something that could exist out there in the world it moves around in. By doing so it simultaneously achieves a kind of self-consciousness of itself. It becomes aware that it exists inside itself the more it is aware that there is an other that exists outside of itself. This makes our amoeba a rather unhappy little fellow, worried about this divided world it is starting to comprehend. Fortunately there comes to the rescue a further stage, in which it starts to appreciate that this very sense of externality only really came into being because of the development of its own consciousness. That doesn't seem so bad and it then becomes a bit more reconciled to this relationship. Once reconciled, it has achieved an increased level of sophistication (at least for an amoeba) which allows it to move upwards a little into a more developed form. It is then prepared to go to the next stage in positing a more complex sense of what exists out there, and so it goes through a similar sequence several times, increasing in sophistication at each stage.

Now what the hell is this author on about – what gives with the amoeba? OK, before you press some button, and, as it were, turn off this book, let me provide a couple of examples that might start to show how and where this could make sense. Take, for example, the relationship between society and law. As a member of our society one might first experience *The Law* as something entirely external: an oppressive force, alien from oneself, that just makes life miserable and stops you having fun. Many teenagers feel like that about *the law*. But over time one might come to appreciate that law doesn't appear out of nothing. That it is your own society which has gradually accumulated a series of procedures that were intended to make social life more bearable. For example, you can have fun without someone breaking a bottle over your head with impunity. If the law is carried out in a way that accords with the original ideals and ideas behind it, then we might, after a while, identify ourselves as citizens who are prepared to be associated with this process and even help develop it further. Some might even contemplate becoming a magistrate. In abstract terms, here is something that we have created, but at first appears to us as an alien, external thing. Over time, once we realize that law exists because we created it, we become reconciled to it. We start to see ourselves in it. Our laws are better than their laws. We may even come to see law as an expression of some force of reason. As we achieve each enhanced level of consciousness about what law is, we mature through this increasingly sophisticated understanding of who and what we are. Ideally we then go on to create better laws.

On the other hand, it is clear that law works partly by having some autonomy from us, the citizens. While that should be positive and is necessary, it also creates a capacity for self-interest that no longer serves, but actually does oppress us. By virtue of this degree of necessary autonomy, law can become merely the means by which lawyers make money, or the threat of being sued so that schools cannot provide medicines to sick children, or the excuse for really boring television shows where a trial is really a trial. In his *Phenomenology*, and as further elaborated in *The Philosophy of Right*, Hegel argues that institutions, such as law, correspond to the manifestation and development of reason itself, as long as they remain true to their original purpose. So *real* education is that which fulfils the reason behind the idea and ideal of education, which is to enhance the capacities of those who are educated. This may not, of course, be the case with what happens to be taught at a particular school. At any given time, although we may make some minor contribution to the development of education or law, it is probably more accurate to say that education and law make us than that we make it. Being brought up within those institutions at a given period, schooled in a particular way, governed in a particular way, helps to make us typical of, say, medieval or nineteenth-century personages, or contemporary Latvians as opposed to Colombians. We are in great measure a product of history.

For Hegel, history consists of a sequence of such processes which we can call dialectical. A society gradually elaborates a custom or institution. Before we achieve law as we know it, we find a series of prior versions: an agreement between groups that, at the place of bartering goods, those taking place in the exchange should not be subject to violence. Then there emerges authority based on religion or kingship, before there develops an autonomous body of law. Similarly, for education, or aesthetics, or commerce or science or religion. But also for clothing, housing, cars and other stuff. OK, we don't have to go all the way back to the amoeba. We can afford to start with humanity's attempts to develop forms by which it comes to understand itself and to develop a world that accords with its sense of reason. However, each such development changes our consciousness and allows us to conceive of a still further development. So now it becomes clear that it isn't really very helpful just to say a person makes law, or that law makes a person. Or to suggest that people make a landscape, or growing up in that landscape makes people. What we end up with is the dynamic process itself, that simultaneously produces that which we colloquially come to talk about as objects and as subjects – medieval peasants and medieval landscapes, both of which are really the products of that same process that we might call medieval times.

But for Hegel there exists one more such process which occupies a rather higher level, and allows us to comprehend all these other processes. That is philosophy. For Hegel, philosophy is the means by which we gain our most advanced consciousness, the one that can comprehend the process I have just described. So the culmination of the history of philosophy is, of course, Hegel's own writings, which finally bring to consciousness this entire history of reason and its increasingly complex manifestations. Hegel saw himself as the final end point of philosophy. It's a rather extravagant claim. But I must admit, I happen to think he was largely right in this. The implication is that most effective philosophy, since his time, is in large measure a rewrite of his arguments. Again, from my limited knowledge of modern philosophy, I am tempted to agree. But I don't mind at all if I am wrong. Because the concern here is not ultimately with Hegel, but with stuff. The philosopher is here just as a means to an end. For this reason the point is not really to remain true to Hegel. We can happily appropriate those ideas that suit our purpose, while ditching others, for example his pseudo-evolutionary view of progress, without so much as an apology to the deceased.

Few people today, even academics outside of philosophy, either read Hegel or are aware of his ideas. But forty years ago a great many people could have spelled out one particular version of these arguments that had come to be the creed followed by half the world. It was Karl Marx who claimed that Hegel had discovered something quite profound, but had made a fundamental mistake in thinking that the key to what humanity produced, or what produced humanity, was intellectual and would be resolved through philosophy. Marx suggested that Hegel had got the process right, but should have looked downwards, rather than upwards, and applied his ideas to our development of the material world. This is what made Marx a materialist. The way he developed from his more orthodox Hegelian roots can be traced in a body of writings variously called the 1844, the Paris, or the Economic and Philosophical manuscripts. These were written by Marx in his twenties (impressive that) but not published until 1932.[14]

For Marx, humanity starts with nature itself. This is the raw material from which we make our lives. Our social evolution consists not of advances in consciousness per se but in our increasing capacity to create an artifactual world from nature, first stone and pot, then agricultural systems, urban life and finally the industrial revolution, which represented a vast acceleration in our capacity to create stuff. But, just as with Hegel, each stage creates a new thing outside of ourselves, and we progress to the extent that we are able to see ourselves in this extension of ourselves, which is after all our own product. The reason we make things is because they potentially extend us as people. But we don't just posit them as external: through an act of consciousness we actually make them through labour. This new material world we have fashioned from nature allows us to travel, to improve our diet, to be entertained, to live longer. More than that, by seeing ourselves in this world we have created, we gain in complexity, sophistication and knowledge. The amoeba (or spore) can now play computer games where they can zap other creatures or turn them into civilizations which conquer other worlds. With these capacities some of us can then develop further our institutions such as education, law and philosophy. If that sounds like hard work, others can just stay there playing games that purport to do this on our behalf. But the initial process is always one of labour. It is human labour that transforms nature into objects, creating this mirror in which we can come to understand who we are. So labour produces culture in the form of stuff.

Marx puts this as follows: 'The object of labour is therefore the objectification of the species-life of man: for man reproduces himself not only intellectually, in his consciousness, but actively and actually and he can therefore contemplate himself in a world he has created.'[15] In reading Marx we have almost bypassed the need to create a theory of culture from Hegel and gone straight to a theory of material culture. There are, however, problems with the way it has been achieved. Hegel saw the process he described, where consciousness creates by positing something outside of itself, as a form of self-alienation. Now I would be the first to admit that the term *self-alienation* sounds more like the aftermath of a awful Saturday night out. But actually for Hegel this was an almost entirely positive and certainly a necessary process for our development.

This process involving self-alienation is what I refer to when I use the word *objectification* subsequently in this book. It is the way we enhance our capacity as human beings. By creating the film industry or cars we can grow ourselves. Every time we do such a thing, by the very same process we also create a contradiction, a possibility of oppressing ourselves if the thing we made then develops its own autonomous interests. By creating the car we also create pollution, road accidents and landscapes devastated by motorways. By creating the film industry we also create Rocky 18, Home Alone 7 and Emmanuelle Meets Godzilla (actually that last one might be worth watching). Nevertheless, we can see that films and cars can be and often are of tremendous benefit, although there is immediately a tension between something we may see as unequivocally good, say an ability to help disabled people get around, as against things we might regard as not so good, such as being encouraged to make polluting journeys to provide profits for the car industry. So within the process of objectification, self-alienating is essential, but it can become just plain alienating.

What is also clear is that, as with clothing in the last chapter, cars, once they exist, become part of what we are. The humanity that existed before roads and traffic jams is not the same as that which exists afterwards. Cars have knock-on effects on other cultural forms. When I find that my family won't let me listen to Nirvana and Hendrix at what I see as the appropriate volume at home, I can blast them out at full volume when driving on a motorway. This is a little bit of what makes me who I am, as are less immediately personal but extremely powerful entailments of cars, such as the oil industry and sometimes war.

The intention here is to replace a theory of stuff as representation with stuff as one part of a process of objectification, or self-alienation. It is the theory that will give theoretical shape to the idea that objects make us, as part of the very same process by which we make them. That ultimately there is no separation of subjects and objects. Instead, in recognition of these thinkers, we can call this a dialectical theory of material culture. Making, growing up with and taking for granted a woven tunic, or fair-trade rice, makes us part of the society that understands itself as a tunic-wearing or fair-trade rice-using society. Making cars manufactures a new version of us. Humanity 4.3 (beta), as it were. But to clarify this further we need to do some backtracking from the direction in which these ideas were taken by Marx.

Marx starts with a vision. Nature of itself belongs to no one. So the things we create from it should be to the benefit of those who are responsible for that creation. Yes, we start with objectification as a process by which we create ourselves. But as Hegel argued, once something is externalized, it can also become oppressive and we can lose consciousness that it ever was our creation. Marx argued that this happens in capitalism, which fools the workers into thinking that what makes this material world is not their labour, but the resources of capital. Even worse, their possession of nature itself is removed as private property. As a result, Marx stops writing much about the second part of the Hegelian process, where we regain this understanding. It gets shunted off into some utopian state called communism. Instead Marx and subsequent Marxists concentrate on this moment of rupture, when consciousness is taken away from us. Objects are reduced to the commodities provided by capitalism. Mostly Marxists used terms such as fetishism, reification and alienation. By now the word objectification has become more literal – subjects turned into objects. It implies that things are no longer fluid, but harden themselves against us to become the instruments of our oppression. By contrast, Hegel saw that we need to accept the integral contradictions to these processes. Private property, where people own and have rights to the place they live in, helps them to identify with that place. It's entirely different from private property where someone owns a property that another person lives in. Clearly stuff can be turned against us and become oppressive, but it is preferable to see this as a contradiction, rather than the only way to characterize our relationship to things. The theory of objectification used here is clearly Hegelian, rather than Marxist. So we still need an alternative route to stuff.

Fortunately Marx was not the only theorist to try and ground Hegel in our material world; he was simply the most influential. Another rather different trajectory is represented by Georg Simmel, one of the founding ancestors of modern sociology. This discussion again is restricted to a few elements of his vast output, *The Philosophy of Money* and some essays he wrote on the concept of culture.[16] While Marx seemed to move us precipitously down from philosophy straight to material culture, Simmel allows us to stop and rest for a moment at the level of a theory of culture. This may be culture in its more particular sense such as art works, or its more general sense, which could then include education or law.

For Simmel, as opposed to Marx, culture itself is inherently tragic, that is, contradictory because, as Hegel argued, it always has this propensity to autonomy. Not just institutions such as education and law, but also stuff itself. Simmel was one of the very very few social theorists who thought deeply about the sheer quantitative increase in stuff that arose during the nineteenth century in which he lived. He could see that quantity, the increase in the amount of stuff we possess, itself posed such a contradiction. We have seen that objectification can be positive. Having more things might provide us with resources that enhance our capacity and experience and understanding. But this doesn't necessarily happen. Consider an individual living on the periphery of commodity culture, say an Australian Aboriginal, now settled into a suburb of Sydney. Their traditional culture had relatively few material things, but was hugely rich in the elaboration of cosmology and kinship. As a student in anthropology I quickly felt tied up in knots just trying to unravel the complexity of Australian Aboriginal kinship systems. We quite properly regard them as rich in culture. However, as individuals drift towards the fringes of urban life, they may lose much of that cultural wealth. But being on the margins, they may have little opportunity to possess, or even to understand, this vast material culture represented by the city. They may end up just reduced to alcoholism.

The way Simmel would have put this is that the subjective only gains when it can assimilate the expanding objective culture. What we cannot assimilate oppresses us. This is potentially just as true for someone born into city life. Simmel wrote several highly influential essays about the contradictions of the metropolis. A place with far more people which allows one to be far more lonely. A place where, if we try and relate to too many things, but have no substantial relationship to any one of them, we can become largely indifferent to the world and to ourselves. It is easy to become blasé in the city. We are then being reduced, rather than expanded, by the sheer quantity of things.

But let's not pretend that the quantity of things is intrinsically oppressive. It is only that it has that capacity to become so. In general, peoples of many societies, who had their own integrity, see the attractions and potentials of this expanded cityscape, and many thrive in it and on it. They bitterly resent anyone telling them that they were better off without it, that they have some responsibility to remain peasants or tribal peoples so that city folk have someone to gawp at on their holidays and anthropologists can claim they are researching something exotic. They have another name for this prior state. They call it poverty. Loads of people around me bemoan some existential loss as a result of having too many things. But I can count the genuine ascetics I know on less than one hand. I simply don't know any at all. The point made by Simmel is not then to see the growth in stuff as intrinsically good or bad, but as intrinsically contradictory.

For Simmel the most significant example of this contradiction was to be found in money itself. Simmel was one of the most eloquent theorists of the positive qualities of money. Money is the basis of modern freedom. Without the capacity to be paid in wages we would have to be apprenticed to other people. Students might have to work for their lecturers directly rather than paying the university. Money is the basis of modern equality. Without it we couldn't have the redistribution of taxation, and the abstract sense of people as equal and quantitative, stripped of their specific qualities that make them unequal. It is that abstraction that permits us even to conceive of equality, whether in voting, in feminism as gender equality, or in using bureaucracy to treat everyone equally. How often do we acknowledge that all such positives depend upon money?

At the same time Simmel can sound rather more like Marx when it comes to the capacity of money to create also inequality as differential possession: to create an abstraction as capital that becomes increasingly divorced from the specifics of things to which we can relate. We are all familiar with a hundred other things we blame money for. This text is being written during a credit crunch crisis, based on the problems of a process called securitization, which is, in effect, a process that simply made capital too abstract for its own good and for our good. But, unlike Marx, Simmel does not separate this off into a period of capitalist money abstraction opposed to a kind of idealized post-commodity communism. Simmel is clear that such contradictions are intrinsic to culture. You simply can't have the benefits of one side of this coin without the risk of the other. Everything we produce has a tendency to autonomous interest and the potential to oppress rather than serve us. If culture, for Simmel, is this Hegelian process that potentially can either grow us or oppress us, then culture is a subset of dialectical philosophy, and material culture is a subset of culture. Stuff has adhering to it this tragic contradiction of culture itself. Commodities are not inherently good or bad, but you can't have their benefits without entailing the risk that they will oppress you. The good news is that awareness of this gives one an opportunity to address this contradiction: to eat, play sports, create transnational corporations, with some potential for moderation.

One of the (many) questions raised by these texts, but especially by this use of Simmel, is whether these ideas only apply to what might be called modern stuff, such as commodities: the deluge that followed from the industrial and consumer revolutions. This is what most people assume. Hegel certainly had a strong modernizing trajectory to his story. But, for an anthropologist, this would be a severe limitation to any theory of material culture, and this would be a very different book about stuff. Remember that Australian Aboriginal stranded on the outskirts of Sydney. It is only too easy to assume that previously he or she possessed, in prior Aboriginal culture, some kind of unsullied, pure, integrated cosmology that contained no contradictions at all. Indeed, this was traditionally the spirit in which much of anthropology was taught. As such, anthropology exhibited a kind of primitivism, but a subtle one. It obviously didn't denigrate other societies, but

it did reduce them to a state of noble savagery whose main purpose
had become a stick with which to beat ourselves. To make us
think of ourselves as people who have lost all culture, and become
merely snivelling victims of vast capitalist and modernist forces:
a dualism that was to a degree reinforced by Marx's black and
white portraits of capitalism and communism.

But in my understanding of Hegel, and then Simmel, stuff is
intrinsically contradictory. Not just our stuff, all stuff. So, for a
brief excursion, let us leave on one side cars and films, and see
what this idea of objectification has to say about the Australian
Aboriginals who had not been resettled in Sydney, with reference
to the work of a Chicago-based anthropologist, Nancy Munn.[17]
Munn's first researches took her to the Walbiri, a group of
Australian Aboriginals who possess relatively little by way of
material culture, at least if we think of stuff as things such as they
carry around for hunting or taking shelter. But, as many studies
have shown, the few mobile objects they use for hunting and
shelters are complemented by an intense relationship with the
landscapes they inhabit: the rock formations, creeks and places
where wallabies are found in abundance.

If most people know anything at all about such Australian
tribes, then they have probably heard of the *dreamtime*; the time
of the ancestors who lie at one remove from people, but whose
actions and consequences remain an integral part of the lives of
the living, ancestors remembered in myth. Stylistically, the myths
of the Walbiri and the writings of Hegel do not appear to have a
whole lot in common. But we can view these myths as at least
analogous to Hegel's philosophy of objectification, just rather
more appropriate to the cosmology of the Walbiri.

Munn studied those myths which described the process by
which ancestral beings created the landscape. They tell how this
too was a process of self-alienation and externalization. There are
three main genres of objectification: metamorphosis, by which an
ancestor transformed his or her whole body into a feature, such
as a hillock; imprinting, by which an ancestor might, for example,
have dug a water hole with his penis; externalization, in which an
ancestor might have taken out from within her body an object
that is now a natural feature of the land. These myths serve for
the Walbiri a similar role to that of history for Hegel. They recognize that there are prior forces which have already created the

world in which we come to be socialized. But in turn we can come to act upon those forces. The Walbiri retain contact with ancestors through the dreamtime and re-enact this relationship in ceremony and ritual today. It is the same landscape and order which is used to legitimate the critical relationships of kinship and social order which give individuals a sense of who they are. So both ancestors and contemporary people externalize themselves as culture and recognize themselves in that which has been created. They objectify. And in their myths they possess also a 'theory' of culture that explains this process.

Many people have heard of the Aboriginal dreamtime, but in the desperate desire to see them as the opposite of ourselves, we are much less aware that Aboriginal societies have an extremely elaborate conceptualization of law.[18] For example, one group may have only the rights to represent a particular action of an ancestor who created some feature in the landscape, while another group has rights over the feature itself. It would be entirely possible to critique Aboriginal systems of law from the perspective of the common critiques of our own law. A feminist, or a communist Aboriginal, could describe these as self-mystifications that delude the tribe into failing to recognize the artificiality of cultural orders that legitimate inequalities of gender or power. The tribe will never achieve equality unless they repudiate them and take up universal human rights. This seems correct. There is surely just as much reification and fetishism in Aboriginal cosmology as in the idea that all profit is justified by risk taking. Such contradictions are fully evident today. These same tribal groups are commonly engaged with concepts of property and universal rights when defending claims made to the state with regard to their own territory or rights over their art works against counterfeits. Land disputes have become something of a major preoccupation. At the same time these peoples may be seeking to limit the penetration of such universalizing languages and laws that could be used to abolish all customary law. If the internal contradictions of their beliefs were not evident before, they certainly are now, in hundreds of contemporary Australian court cases.

If the Walbiri exemplify objectification within one group, then the next region studied by Munn illustrates the process by which society creates itself through objectification within a wider cultural sphere. This was the Kula ring, famously described by

Malinowski in his 1922 book *Argonauts of the Western Pacific*,[19] from the vantage point of one of its component island groups, the Trobriand Islands. What fascinated Malinowski, and continues to entrance us today, was finding that a whole series of island groups, off the coast of New Guinea, have formed themselves into a kind of circuit. This did not depend upon knowledge of the circuit as a whole but on the more immediate relationship between neighbouring groups that constituted the circuit. Around this ring circulated valuables, especially armshells in one direction and necklaces in the other direction. Munn undertook her research in an island called Gawa in which people contribute canoes that are used in this inter-island exchange. She traces how various kin relationships work through exchanges of labour and food to facilitate the construction of these canoes. Since the canoes are then launched into the Kula, one could see this as the alienation of the relationships and the labour that went into their production. But, in return for the canoes, these people receive valuables, which have been the product of similar processes elsewhere. These valuables are then traded downwards back through the same sets of relationships that produced the canoes.

The question behind all this is, frankly, why bother? Why not just sit at home and watch television, or at least sunsets? After all it clearly wasn't just to give research material to anthropologists. In her book *The Fame of Gawa*, Munn elaborates on this necessity. A couch potato (or couch yam) amongst the Gawa people would be someone who just wanted to grow yams and then eat them, without all this Kula ring palaver. The Gawa have a pretty effective response to this. They accuse their couch potatoes of witchcraft. If you just grow food and eat it, then no culture is created. If, by contrast, you grow food, exchange it in complex networks that create canoes, send these in turn to be exchanged for valuables from other islands, representing other networks, then something big happens. What comes back is a value, which Munn translates as Fame. An elaborate field is created through which people and islands grow not just food; they grow reputation, they can become Argonauts and have adventures, stories can be told, things heard about and seen. Life is richer. Witchcraft is that which shrinks and shrivels, not just bellies but also horizons, while exchange, such as Kula, allows people to grow fat with fame and fortune. Through exchange people learn how to 'get a life'.

Seen from this vantage, objectification, the process of self-alienation, externalization and return, becomes a theory of what we can call culture, as much for Gawa as for Simmel's Berlin. But these are still pressures that can oppress people, especially couch potatoes. And if there weren't any such people, there probably wouldn't be all these sanctions of witchcraft. I have met loads of unhappy people in what are called tribal and village societies who could be said to find their own culture oppressive. Something we prefer to ignore in simple versions of us and them.

A central role in this process called culture turns out to be that subset we can now properly call material culture. The Kula, at one level, is simply a circuit around which people circulate objects such as armshells and necklaces. It's not just people who become famous through their adventures in Kula. Individual shells gain their own reputation because of the travels they have passed through and then people strive to ensure that famous objects pass through their hands and not those of a rival. One of the most influential foundational theories for the discipline of anthropology is a simplified version of this theory. Mauss, partly influenced by Malinowski, wrote an essay on the gift.[20] He suggested that the basis of most relationships is debt. That in giving something to another, whether a necklace, or one's sister as a wife, a bond is created between the society of givers and that of receivers. The bond consists of the obligation to return this gift. Not to remain in debt. The Maori have their own conceptualization of the force which lies in the object itself and creates the obligation to return the debt. This concept of *hau* is perhaps the most debated of all anthropological models. It seems analogous to a notion of the inalienable, that which is never really given away, because it demands some sort of return. If you give me something and I feel obliged one day to give something back, then we are in a relationship. It may be supportive or it may be competitive, but it is a relationship. Once again, in this theory of the gift, we do not start from what societies do with things, it is the circulation of things that creates society. Or better still, what we call society and stuff are actually artificial separations out of the same process. It may be a person that is given as gift; are they then an object? Or is it better sometimes to dissolve the distinction?

Simmel marvelled at the incredible diversity of experience possible in a contemporary city, but marvelled even more at an individual's capacity to blithely ignore the same, or to be oppressed by it. The accusation of witchcraft suggests that, just because there is the Kula ring doesn't mean that an individual islander might not wish to escape from it. We cannot assume every wife 'swapped' in gift exchange in order to facilitate the reproduction of dominant kinship obligations feels comfortable, just as we cannot assume she doesn't. Objectification is a dialectical theory of culture, not just capitalist culture, because contradiction is not just a new feature of modern capitalism, or an aspect of living in cities. It is intrinsic to the very process we describe as culture.

Still, creating culture is a pretty extraordinary process and it does indeed make anthropologists happy. The Walbiri provided an example of objectification within one group, the Kula the creation of a kind of super-group. Culture is contradictory rather than completely prescriptive. The Kula exists, but some Gawans become famous Argonauts, and others sit at home, put their feet up and risk being seen as a witch. To make these points we have climbed up from stuff, to culture to dialectical philosophy: to a peak in which the distinction of subjects and objects has disappeared. But the air is thin up there and it is cold and lonely. Most of the time we probably prefer talking what we generally term common sense, and being what philosophers (and others) might regard as extremely vulgar. In everyday life, sitting in a pub over a drink, we might prefer to be in conversations where there are clear and unproblematic entities to be called people and things, and we can tell the difference. That people act on and are represented or symbolized by things. We converse in all those ways which this chapter has suggested may be in some measure wrong. But this is a discrepancy to explore rather than ignore. For one thing, going up the philosophy mountain is great for a quick revelation as to how things 'really' are, but we wouldn't want to live up there. But, before we are ready to clamber back down we have one final peak to climb.

Materiality

So far this chapter has shown that it is possible to have a theory of things, such as framing, and secondly how to progress towards a dialectical theory of objectification that transcends things and persons. But for a topic called stuff, we also need to tackle a third aspect, which is the meaning and implications of materiality itself.[21] The problem with materiality is that for some reason we seem on the whole to be not at all keen on it. There is an underlying principle to be found in most of the religions that dominate recorded history. Wisdom has been accredited to those who claim that materiality represents the merely apparent, behind which lies that which is real. Perhaps the most systematic development of this belief arose over two millennia within South Asia. For religions such as Buddhism and Hinduism, theology has been centred upon the critique of materiality. At its simplest Hinduism, for example, rests upon the concept of *maya*, which proclaims the illusory nature of the material world. The aim of life is to transcend the apparently obvious; the stone we feel through the sole of our shoe, or the body as the core of our sensuous existence. Truth comes from our apprehension that this is mere illusion.

Nevertheless, paradoxically, material culture has been of considerable consequence as the means of expressing this conviction. In a Hindu temple the merely vestigial forms at the centre of a temple may be contrasted with the massive gates at the periphery. The sari of an elderly woman in its faded pastels presents a stark contrast to the bright and sensual sari of the bride. It thereby expresses, in material form, the goal of transcending our attachment to material life. So, to start on this seemingly vast question of what is materiality, we had better admit that, whatever materiality is, it is something we often profoundly don't want to be.

Yet the history of South Asia is not just the history of its religions. There is a parallel history, which tells of the endless struggle of cosmology with practice. This is the history of accumulation, taxation, wars and looting, empire and excess. It culminates in the integration of this region within a global political economy in which politics is increasingly subservient to an economics whose premise with respect to materiality could hardly be more different. In economic thought the accumulation of material commodities is itself the source of our extended capacity as humanity. Poverty is defined as the critical limit to our ability to realize ourselves as persons, consequent upon a lack of commodities. The focus upon materiality, though here in the form of accumulation, is therefore just as strong in economics as it is in Hinduism.

For a discipline such as anthropology, that is concerned with what it is to be human, we need therefore to start our discussion of this issue with an acknowledgement that the definition of humanity has often become almost synonymous with the position taken on the question of materiality. A good deal of what people take to be morality has followed in the wake of this. So either we desperately want to escape being material, or we spend our lives trying to accumulate more material or, most bizarrely, virtually all the people I live amongst in London seem to want to do both of these things simultaneously.

If world religions and global economics depend on their stance to materiality, then its investigation is clearly not just a minor indulgence of material culture studies as a subsection of anthropology. Hinduism and economics are not just beliefs about the world, but vast institutional forces that try to ensure that people live according to their tenets through priesthoods or through structural adjustment programmes. In this respect capitalism and several major religions are equal and analogous attempts to impose particular positions on materiality. On a somewhat smaller but still significant scale, materiality is obviously important to the study of media, the definition of art, the creation of new financial instruments, environmental politics and the respect we have for persons.

We will never get far in understanding materiality if we blunder into it head on. Let me remind you of my original stricture against trying to define stuff. Is a hard thing, such as a stone, more material than a soft thing such as a bubble? Is an idea that lasts more material than one that doesn't? It's that pedantic semantics again. It may be that in physics one can define materiality, but the definition would be of little value to social science. What we can do instead is to see what people in practice mean by this idea. What do religions which want to escape the material world do about it; how do people in practice employ ideas of more or less materiality? The following is a précis of some papers in an edited book on the subject of materiality that each provides us with examples we can use to think more deeply about what is at stake here.

We can start by returning to the fundamental contradiction whereby religions find that the best way to express immateriality is through materiality. It's hard not to be entranced by the ancient Egyptians, largely because materiality is something at which they were spectacularly good. What we are entranced by are a trilogy of mummies, pyramids and monuments. Meskell tells us what they thought they were doing when they created these things in the first place.[22] The ancient Egyptians believed, for example, that one helped give life to the gods by creating the precise statue appropriate to them. Similarly one gave extended life to the individual by getting the process of mummification right. Sheer materiality, expressed as one of the great pyramids, gave the very sense of 'being' a precise shape and form. So we are impressed by the legacy of their stuff. And yet, just as with Hinduism or Christianity, this cosmology rested upon a belief in the inherent superiority of the immaterial world. So the ancient Egyptians express our paradox with particular clarity. In essence it was their faith in the potential of monumentality to express immateriality that has created their legacy as a material presence in our own world. We continue to be enthralled by statues, mummies and pyramids because of the very exuberant faith that the Egyptians put into the process of materialization as a means for securing their own immortal transubstantiation.

If the ancient Egyptians express one logical implication of this paradox, then thanks to Engelke we can explore another,[23] this time through following the logic of a contemporary religious group, the Apostolic Christians of Zimbabwe. In a way this has been a long time coming. The very founding of Protestantism saw thousands of people slain over esoteric arguments as to what exactly we mean by immateriality. Whether wine and bread were actually the blood and body of the Christian messiah or merely their representation. Whether churches should be full of icons as in Counter-Reformation churches, or entirely stripped of them. Ever since the Reformation there have been movements within Protestantism that have tended towards iconoclasm and asceticism as attempts to foreground the importance of immateriality to spirituality.

The Masowe Apostolics, studied by Engelke, take this to its logical conclusion in several respects. They feel that it has now become obvious that prior Christian forms failed in their quest for transcendence because they were betrayed by the very materiality of things such as bibles and churches. Protestantism had failed to follow through on its own logic of spirituality. So these Apostolics meet in fields rather than churches and memorize their teachings rather than holding forth with a bible. They try to repudiate systematically every material object that seems to mediate their relation to their Christ, so that they can achieve ultimately an unmediated relationship, soul to spirit. Yet even they cannot fully adhere to this ideal. The passion to repudiate things per se leads them to attach still more importance to the very few objects that remain to them. Engelke writes a whole essay on the ambiguity surrounding sacred honey and the constant temptation to use this lapse of immaterialism, the fact that they do see something special in honey, as a conduit that brings spiritual power back down to our instrumental earth.

So, the other side to the coin of materiality is immateriality – literally in the cases of the coinage analysed by Maurer.[24] In religion the main purpose of the material is to express the immaterial. So, for a deeply religious Islamic society money is more important as a means to comprehend divinity than as a means to facilitate secular exchange. This is why in the early caliphate a consequence of the replacement of the Caliph's head by Qur'anic inscriptions on coins is the subordination of the issue of representation in coinage to that of the technologies for the imagination of the divine. The way a coin faces both sides, upwards to the transcendent and downwards to the functionalism of the market, is utilized to give words themselves (as in calligraphy) a role in objectification. The coin helps the believer to conceive of this Janus-faced relationship. Maurer argues that the effect of the new coinage is to bring the issue of how one understands the deity down to the somewhat safer question of how one understands the coinage. At the same time this secures the authority of coinage. In effect such a society has, by making coins a mode for the apprehension of the divine, thereby 'leveraged' their coinage as value, with the backing of divine authority. By removing the face of the coin it has actually 'countenanced' by the word. Once again, there are contemporary implications. Maurer's other example is the growth in Islamic banks that attempt to ensure that business operates in such a way that it declares its obeisance to religious strictures rather than stands in opposition to it.

So we can start with this paradox by which the immaterial can only be expressed through the material. We then find that most people prefer a gradation between these two, rather than a stark dualism. Some things and some people should be seen as more material than others. This is very well established in Hinduism as generally practised. In India we find a hierarchy starting from the mass of small and disparate images of regional spirits and divinities. These have been incorporated into the larger pantheon of Hindu deities. The minor deities are incorporated into mainstream religion by being viewed as *avatars*, expressive manifestations of the major deities such as Siva and Vishnu. The major deities in turn are seen by some as aspects of the one supreme deity. At higher philosophical levels the idea of a deity is seen as itself a vulgar rendition of a more transcendent sense of enlightenment, for those whose consciousness can achieve such heights. For them the very notion of God is a necessary simplification of something still less material.

So one can correctly label Hinduism as polytheistic, monotheistic and even atheistic, partly because each is seen as appropriate to the capacity of certain kinds of people to apprehend the 'reality' behind mere materiality. Ordinary people are ordinary partly because they require more materiality. Great sages are great partly because they can apprehend more immateriality. So if deities form a hierarchy, so do people. The lowly are those who need minor spirits, with more human-like foibles and myths, in order to help them comprehend religious ideals. By contrast, at the apex are the intellectual sages, who can contemplate transcendence in a more purely philosophical idiom.

So what helps us to understand materiality would not be a physicist's demonstration that monuments are more densely material than sponges in some absolute sense. What we employ is our sense of such a gradation between more or less material. Rowlands shows how some persons also can be seen as more material than others, by the people of the Cameroon grassfields.[25] Appropriate metaphors abound – some persons and objects are seen as weighty, others are slight. Some people loom large, even when we might have preferred that they didn't. Others, however hard they try to gain our attention, we manage to leave at the periphery of our vision. For these people in Cameroon a chief has particular density. Materiality is gained by substances through the process of circulating through his body and presence. So, for example, his spit is itself efficacious in changing the order of things. By contrast, his subjects strive to have a presence as persons, but they simply do not possess the reality granted to the body of the chief. All other bodies are mere shadows of the one real body. Rowlands notes how these people had a parallel encounter with colonialism. They found new modes, such as bureaucratic form filling, which made some people more material than others, in relation to this alternative source of power. While Meskell indicates the extraordinary gulf between the God-like and ordinary in death and the afterlife, Rowlands draws our attention to the assertion of such distinctions in life. Sometimes people try to manipulate this aspect of themselves – consider the way a size zero model has more presence than a size eight.

Many of us live in a world where more and more people are quite distant from any cosmology identified with established religion. But our secular world is just as haunted today by shadowy spirits that seem to perform strange magical feats that conjure vast powers out of the dross. People such as the Japanese traders in derivatives markets, studied by Mayazaki,[26] are surely at least as incomprehensible to the uninitiated as any theological discussion of Talmud or the Sutras. Key processes in contemporary finance start not with doing something, but with an act of re-conceptualization. The most fundamental process is called securitization. This is the process that turns a potential future profit stream into something that can be traded. In turn, a derivative may be formed by trading the risk involved in speculating on what that profit stream will be. This sounds obscure enough, but what is deeply unsettling is to contemplate what is thereby produced.

In the trading known as arbitrage, experts will use models derived from theoretical physics to note tiny discrepancies between how a market should operate according to these models and how it is actually operating. But trading on the 'as though they existed' is sufficient to make these values exist. A million units can thereby be traded as a billion units. Well more, actually. The rabbits coming out of these hats reproduce at a rate that would even astonish rabbits. The notional amounts of derivatives contracts by the year 2000 were already more than a hundred trillion dollars, a figure most of us can no longer convert into a meaningful image. During a credit crunch it can even more magically be transformed back into a mere puff of smoke.

Now for present purposes you don't have to understand modern finance (though perhaps we really should). The point is merely that the relationship between materiality and immateriality is no more straightforward in secular than in religious domains. Clearly this vast sum exists in some sense, but in what sense? Has derivative trading materialized something that didn't exist, or is it largely a juggling of immaterial concepts? One of the neat things about the Japanese arbitrage traders studied by Miyazaki is that they don't get paid by some share of the money they make in this trading. They accept a standard wage, because they see themselves as doing a good deed in the world. By spotting these discrepancies in the way markets operate, they are in a way punishing its imperfections, and in some small way helping to perfect the market itself. To make it as pure as its models. Is this then the secular opposite of religion? Hardly. Actually, religions were pretty good at making money on occasion also.

The volume on materiality, from which these case studies are drawn, contains many more examples of these paradoxical and ironic implications of the term. What they demonstrate is the varied and concrete consequences of this initial paradox. The more humanity reaches towards the conceptualization of the immaterial, the more important the specific form of its materialization. It's the same reason why modern art seems to sell for more money, the more it succeeds in its claim to esoteric conceptualization. If a work of art can fully encapsulate a politically radical repudiation of capitalism and materialism, it's probably worth a small fortune. We are not trying to assault common sense for the sake of it. All these examples show that contradiction and paradox and complexity are integral parts of the ordinary world we live in and essential to understanding it.

This chapter is by no means trying to exhaust the potential of theoretical approaches to materiality and to stuff. The theoretical perspectives that have been expounded here can hopefully complement, rather than be seen as in some kind of competition with many other significant developments in thinking about material culture. There are differences. Bruno Latour,[27] for example, seems convinced that dialectical theory merely resurrects the opposition of subjects and objects, while I believe it succeeded in transcending them. Influential alternatives within anthropology include the work of Alfred Gell,[28] who, as with Latour, found a route to transcending the opposition of things and persons through an emphasis on the way objects can be said to have agency, although Gell uses this to create an approach to art. Also influential are various versions of phenomenology, espoused, for example, by anthropologists such as Ingold and Tilley.[29] Reading these additional approaches will provide a much broader, and more insightful, understanding of the possible ways in which we can go beyond our natural dualism of persons and things than would be achieved by reading this book alone. One of the trends in the work of some of these other anthropologists, which seems entirely appropriate, is to look more at substances such as stone or wood rather than, as in this volume, thinking of stuff mainly as artefacts or things.

What all such approaches have in common is the desire to give greater attention and respect to materiality and material culture. Yet they all work in relation to a discipline that in Europe is conventionally described as social anthropology, not just as anthropology. This raises one final issue – the potential opposition, not between subjects and objects, but between social science and material culture. The possibility of a modern social science, such as anthropology, was at the least secured with the radical secularism that viewed religion as the emanation of the social collective. If there is a single founding ancestor to Western social science, it is probably Durkheim who most clearly enunciated this belief.[30] The premise was a secularism that saw God and religious rules as fabrications. Societies had invented such beliefs and invented God because they needed to represent themselves to themselves. Religion was a collective social representation. But at the same moment that this theory desacralized religion by seeing it as fabrication, it actually also sacralized the social. The social sciences become devoted to the study of all phenomena that stand for what we now call society, social relations or indeed simply the subject.

The reason was simple enough. Durkheim felt that we could manage without God as long as we believed in society. Mere individuals bereft of this collective identity would lose a sense of purpose to life, as implied in his study of suicide. The problem, from the point of view of something that could have been called material culture studies, was not just that persons and societies were put on this semi-divine pedestal, but that this was achieved through distancing them from the vulgarity of the material. In this tradition, the study of persons' relationships to things should always finally be reduced back to social relations. This was not Durkheim's doing. In fact, as was previously noted, his compatriot

Mauss was highly respectful of the potency of things in his analysis of the gift. This anti-materialism was something that long pre-dates Durkheim. It was rather the abiding legacy of the roots of this secular ideal of society in religion itself. As we have seen, religion constantly achieved its ideal of transcendence through its repudiation of the material. Enlightenment is tantamount to the separation from desire. When we look at ourselves today, we can see we have inherited much the same system of beliefs. The one thing we are never supposed to be is materialistic, because it is assumed that paying attention to the material is always at the expense of paying attention to the social, to the person. This will be a major theme in the companion to this volume, *Consumed by Doubt*.

This is also why approaches to material culture have tended to be held in some disdain by mainstream anthropology. The reason goes right back to the start of this chapter when my Indian informants watched me paying inordinate attention, as a PhD student, to pots and tried to persuade me that I had missed the point or indeed the plot. To pay too much attention to things is seen as a diminution in our capacity to appreciate persons as persons. Yet most secular people believe that the dethronement of God, the previous essential guarantor of morality, released, rather than suppressed, the development of a modern ethical sensibility.

The question is, after a couple of hundred years of secularism, whether we still need such a highfalutin ideal of society to help deal with the trauma of replacing the divinity. Indeed perhaps keeping that aura of the divine and attributing it to society has been more a problem than an asset? Personally I would rather have a divine God than pay obeisance to society as a kind of divine-lite. It could well be that the dethronement of society or humanity, or social relations or the subject, can be the premise for the further development of modern ethics, not its dissolution. This should not be confused with any opposition to society as an analytical term, as against, for example, the individual. There is very little in this book that would support a conceptualization of individuals outside of social relationships and indeed society. But we can speak of society, appreciate it, applaud it and work for it, without reifying it.

So if the first revolution consisted of Durkheim's enthroning society in the stead of religion, we now look to gain maturity by burying the corpse of our imperial majesty, society. Objects no longer have to be constantly reduced to subjects. But there is no reason at all for placing material culture on the pedestal that now looks empty. Academic work is best done from the more modest position of feet on the ground. But we can achieve this modesty partly through a greater acceptance of our own materiality as well as that of the world. Not materiality made exotic by the wondrous achievements of science, nor made criminal by the curses of environmentalists, though stuff has its achievements and its costs. But the emphasis in this chapter is on simply making stuff ordinary, as part and parcel of our existence in the world.

3

Houses: Accommodating Theory

Housing and Power

One of the delights of dialectical theory, alongside its cultivation of extremism, is that it includes within itself clear strictures about what one should do with theory. No one drives you further to the upper reaches of theoretical ambition than Hegel. There you will find ideas about Absolute Reason that can explain even more than *The Hitchhiker's Guide to the Galaxy* about life, the Universe and the rest of it (though I never found anything in Hegel about the number 42). But to be consistent, dialectical theory must imply that just theory alone, like everything else humanity produces, will always tend to become destructive and follow its own interests, oppressing rather than serving humanity. Unless there is a counter-movement that (to use its own terminology) negates this abstraction and brings it back into the service of our interests and welfare.

This is often the case. Theory, philosophy, modern art, economics and other movements that utilize obscure abstractions can easily degenerate into pretentious obfuscation and become oppressive playgrounds of academic divas and elites used to intimidate as much as to impress. Academics, tempted by the promise of an easy and assured claim to cleverness, create vast circulations of obscure and impressive citations. A scattering of names such as Lacan or Deleuze and Guattari is usually a good sign of such oppressive conceits. It is only through the subsequent processes of maturing and re-grounding theory in its application to everyday lives and languages that such cleverness becomes transformed into understanding and re-directed to a compassionate embrace, rather than an aloof distaste. To make matters worse, the most oppressive use of theory tends to come dressed in the guise of critical or radical political endeavour, a claimed concern with the actually oppressed conditions of our humanity.

So the task now is to take our artistic-looking idealized theory, once white marble, nowadays more angular perspex, and drag it back into the mud and murk of everyday life until it looks a lot less intimidating and more like something we feel at ease with bringing home to the folks. In this chapter the device for bringing theory home is through immersing it in the more general problem of what a home actually is. The aim is literally to domesticate theory, to help us feel at home with these abstractions by showing that the theoretical ideas discussed in the previous chapter can deliver genuine insights into how we ordinarily feel at home in this vast world. So, while less explicit in address to theory, this chapter also starts with issues of objectification and moves on to questions of agency and materiality.

Clothing raised the issue of the superficial, and our discussion proceeded through a substantive analysis of how we dress to demonstrate how clothing and persons mutually constitute each other. To a rather greater degree than clothing, housing implicates contours of power and scale that make such intimate issues as our personal relationships often contingent upon much grander forces. We are thereby confronted with a much broader and deeper context for our analysis. Consider the relationship between people and their homes in London. Just as in the case of clothing, people in London might want their homes to be part of a similar process of mutual constitution. But very often, if this is what they desire, it is a thwarted desire because housing brings with it powerful forces which are by no means under their control. I may have just made critical comments about the purity of certain academic radical politics, but I have no desire to eschew politics and my colours are firmly nailed to the mast of unashamedly left-orientated politics, whose values and core lie in a desire for equality of welfare.

The issues with clothing are simplified because, while there is a major fashion industry out there, we still retain a good deal of choice and autonomy with respect to both selecting and wearing clothes. Basically clothes are relatively cheap. But houses are altogether different. Houses are the elephants of stuff. Huge lumbering beasts that are excessively hard to control. You can buy a sweater at Primark for £8 but to return with it to your own house in London will cost you more like £300,000. As a result, property attracts a great many more interested parties: the state, landholders, local councils, building societies and the like. Against these forces, any desire by us, the mere people who dwell in houses, to engage in a certain relationship to them can find us way down any pecking order of power. Sometimes these powers manifest themselves in quite extraordinary and unexpected ways, hidden within genres of material culture where we do not perceive them as power. This chapter therefore deals much more directly with issues of power than chapter 1. Beginning with the larger forces that operate on houses, such as global ideologies, it then moves downwards to smaller worlds of power and difference, expressed in gender and other relationships.

To start from the widest context, we have lived for quite some time now in a period of global housing, in that there are trends and forces that have radically determined housing stock in every part of the world. This includes the architecture of much of London's structures over the twentieth century.[1] Earlier it was suggested that philosophy, often in collusion with art, has a tendency to clamber all over us in its zeal and thereby become oppressive. One instance of this came with the rise of modernism in the early part of the twentieth century. Stimulated by the advances of science, liberated by the repudiation of past convention by the arts, modernism forged its own proclamations of how the future should and would look. With respect to housing this was not some slight fashion that came and went. Marshalled by the zealotry of Le Corbusier and the Bauhaus, it became itself the orthodoxy of architecture and design. Façade was a crime, form would follow function. Houses would be honest, objective and rational, and if need be even brutal. As an instrument of objectification, this new architecture would liberate its inhabitants, who would themselves become modern in the mirror of their new environment. Liberated from dusty crevices of history, exposed by shiny white surfaces, we would come to see so much more clearly who we could be.

We saw in the last chapter that, left to itself, stuff tends to modesty. There is a natural humility to things, in that they work best as the frame that guides our sense of what is appropriate, rather than as things we pay regard to in their own right. This tendency can make stuff quite powerful when put into the service of ideology. When someone tells us we should do this or be that, we bridle and feel put upon. When this message is carried, not by a hectoring voice, but well hidden within the mere substance of apparently silent stuff, we are less likely to sense our disempowerment. So it was in the early twentieth century. Officially politicians and the voice of ideology were engaged in continual battles of right as against left, socialism and the market. These we knew about and could contest. Yet, over exactly the same period, there grew up new modernist tower blocks to house the new modernist populations. Curiously, they did not listen to, or obey, these official distinctions between states and markets, between communism and capitalism. All the explicit contests of ideology were avoided. As a result, the spread of modernist architecture swept blissfully onwards regardless. It made not one iota of difference whether you were living in New York or Moscow. You were equally likely to be seeing a transformation of the urban landscape as it was taken over by modernism. These objects were vast, but we didn't see them nearly as clearly as expressions of official or political ideology.

Yet while forces did not marshal themselves on conventional lines of communism against capitalism, there was another remarkably quiet battle taking place around the field of architecture. Vast movements of resistance started to gather their forces to prevent modernism taking over the planet, yet very few people were even aware that such a war was being waged. Even in retrospect, we fail to pay regard to the evidence. We may even be mistaken as to who won. It is easy to think that modernity became ubiquitous as the form and style of modern housing. After all, it didn't just appear in the clusters of residential tower blocks. It was equally dominant in schools, offices and hospitals, replacing crenellations and spires with glass and concrete. But modernism isn't ubiquitous, and wandering around the streets of London one starts to realize that finally it was almost entirely confined to the housing that was directly built by the state and corporations.

Come off the main road and wander around the interior streets of London and one finds that, apart from state housing built for workers, most of the privately built housing stock looks very different. It looks like suburbia. Who was the Le Corbusier of suburbia? Who rallied the population and told them to build barricades of bay windows, pebbledash and porches against the predation of this modernist beast? Well, no one. And yet if we interrogate these streets we can once again find they tell of an ideology just as consistent in its logic as that of modernism. After all, can it be coincidence that we are looking at the *half*-timbered, *semi*-detached, *sub*-urban dwellings of the *middle* classes? These terms are redolent of ambiguity and a refusal to choose between alternative categories. As Mary Douglas argued, we dislike such ambivalence; it seems unprincipled and it is no wonder that officially this style was condemned. Yet the more that authoritative discourses described suburbia as ugly and conservative and irrational, the more it flourished. Following the expansion of the London underground system, there were created a proliferation of suburban colonies that prided themselves on façade and insisted on at least some attempt to add cottage front gardens to urban homes, that brought the country Cotswolds to Finchley. Just to reinforce the point, they were buttressed from the inside by cocktail cabinets and dressers. Steel and science and rationality had no chance against doorknobs and Dunroamin. Le Corbusier had no defence ready against *nice* and *pretty*.

The turning point for the UK came in 1968 with an accidental explosion in a residential tower block called Ronan Point, which revealed certain structural faults. And the struggle was largely over by the time that block was demolished in 1986. By this time, the same official voices that had so decried suburbia now directed their ire against these modernist residential blocks. Politicians of both right and left, who once rivalled each other in their desire to build such blocks, now united in their condemnation of high rise public housing, especially when it took the form of state-owned estates. Seen as a social failure, the people who lived there were increasingly regarded as urban detritus, responsible for everything that was bad about city life. Modern housing blocks bred crime and alcoholism. Yet who actually built these estates?

Who had destroyed endless rows of small houses, condemned as slums, and replaced them with this vision of community that was supposed to rise inevitably from the careful construction by architects of an appropriate balance of communal and private space? It was never the people who lived within these dwellings; their opinions had never been solicited or voices heard. The people being condemned as urban failures had never been consulted in the decision to move them into such dwellings. They were being castigated by the very people who had made those decisions, the planners, council leaders and bureaucrats. People who actually ran the state and built modernist architecture, but who curiously when it came to their own private lives (apart from architects themselves) tended to prefer to live in semi-detached or even detached housing.

Taken as a potted history of twentieth-century London housing, this appears a far cry from my mutually constituted collusions of persons and things happily making each other. It's almost the opposite. When first analysed this case study was intended as an exemplification of the Marxist concept of ideology. In that tradition, ideology stood for a paradox; that as a process of objectification people may well understand themselves in the mirror of the world they live within. But what happens when that world is created by others, rather than by themselves? If they see themselves in that world, then it would follow that they now misunderstand themselves. One powerful class built houses to objectify their own values, but also built the housing that came to represent the values against which they defined themselves. So, as in accordance with the Marxist concept of ideology the mass of the population were forced to see themselves in the mirror of the stuff produced by a dominant class, not their own stuff. Except that, contrary to Marxist assumptions, neither the proletariat nor the ruling class won the day. If anything, it was the middle class of suburbia, a class so universally derided by theorists that no one had bothered to theorize them properly.

This exemplifies the way housing can provide a critical caveat to the points made earlier about clothing. Yes, people are constructed by their material world, but often they are not themselves the agents behind that material world through which they must live. As we bring our theory of objectification back to the everyday world of housing, it's already looking pretty dirty; though perhaps muddled as much as muddy. Yet this is not a simple tale of recognizable villains and class interests. While right and left were equal in their zeal to build and their zeal to condemn, they need not have been conscious of the likely consequences of their actions. To find these values objectified in housing, you don't get very far by asking people, you have to examine the logic of the stuff itself, the form and underlying order of the built environment.

Within this example there is an architecture of modernism that spoke stridently of its stance to the world; and an architecture of suburbia that remained quiet and demure with respect to any underlying message. A material culture analysis has to listen to the explicit voices, but remain focused on messages that appear like invisible ink, emerging only under the wash of analysis. So far we have addressed only the exterior of houses, the way they face the public domain. If we want to consider issues of power on a more intimate scale we need to cross the thresholds and enter inside, to look beyond façades to the process of interior decoration. Here we will find another field of struggle. But inside and outside the house are hardly entirely separate domains. The two remain deeply entwined, as the next case study will illustrate. Indeed for the time being we will stay with the urban modernist state housing of London, but look inside to see how that helps us re-think the meaning of this term objectification in relation to power.[2] So let's pass through the living rooms and settle down to a cup of tea in the kitchen. After all, this is a working-class estate in North London, and tea in the kitchen is a proper place to have such a chat.

As you sit nursing your tea (coffee if you insist), reflect on the kitchens themselves. Since this was built as a single estate, under modernist guidance, the likelihood is that all the original tenants who moved in on completion of the building would have been allocated a flat with pretty much the identical kitchen to their neighbours'. So you could imagine this population as artists. Each is presented with a blank canvas – a white kitchen surface. After around thirteen years, at the time of my study, what had they painted onto this canvas and why? In particular I wanted to know whether some people had made radical changes and others not, and whether we could account for this difference in their ability to appropriate the things which they were allocated by the state.

In most cases there were considerable changes, but the explanation for these was not simple. The kitchen fitments provided by the state were actually quite good in quality. I consulted with an expert in ergonomics to establish this and also to confirm that when residents replaced them with expensive fitments, purchased from shops, they thereby gained no functional advantage. According to this expert, the newly purchased items were not ergonomically superior. Since these people were tenants, and not owners, they also gained no financial advantage by such a replacement – this was not an investment. So replacing one's kitchen with expensive new fittings does not seem to manifest some obvious form of rationality. But, at the other extreme, there were also kitchens that after thirteen years presented the very same decorative scheme that had originally been present when the flats were first occupied. But this did not mean the tenants had never undertaken decorative work. It often meant that when, every few years, they needed to re-paint their properties, they had chosen to retain this original style and appearance. Again there is no functional reason why they should choose to do so.

To understand what these artists had or had not done to their blank canvases we need to start with their very definite relationship to power represented by the state. This was a time when the UK government, under Margaret Thatcher, scorned to hide its disdain for state housing and tended to stigmatize those who occupied such flats. It was one of the reasons the people who lived there had come to believe that the kitchen fitments they had been supplied with couldn't possibly be any good and needed replacing. There is nothing intrinsically demeaning in living in state housing or renting rather than home ownership. In plenty of other countries rented accommodation may be preferred or even celebrated. But in the UK, at that time, these tenants were at the tail end of the story just told, where they were being blamed for the failures of modernist architects. Typically this estate had received awards when it was first built, but by now was seen as the pits. Under such conditions it is hardly surprising that for these families the flats themselves almost felt like the presence of an enemy. Simply by living there, they found they were branded with this now stigmatized identity of council tenants. This was not at all helped by the attitudes of local councils at that time. The bureaucracy remained extremely prohibitive about tenants doing anything that represented a major change to their flats. The local council had come to possess a big brother element that seemed to be in control of every last detail of one's life. In this modernist prison any change you made to the flat was seen as an attack on the architectural harmony of the whole. All of these factors meant that the relationship between people and the place they lived in reeked of alienation.

If this was the starting point that people were desperate to go beyond, the next question was which of them had been successful in their struggle and why? It appeared that the most important resource people had in changing their relationship to their own accommodation was not money. After all, it costs exactly the same amount to re-paint the original colours of the kitchen as to paint new colours on the walls. Very few people had actually gone out to purchase entirely new kitchens. Mostly it was a case of superficial decorations such as ornaments, posters and calendars on walls. These were used to extensively personalize some flats, but not all. What soon became clear was that the people who had been able to carry out this transformation were those who had good social relations and the support of others. This was the first of what became many studies of material culture, which concluded that it was the people blessed with strong relationships to other people that also had effective and fulfilling relationships to the material world, while those who felt they had failed in their relationships to either things or persons also tended to be unable to construct satisfactory relationships in the other domain. This was an important conclusion since it was the very opposite of that common assumption made in accusations of materialism, a word that implies that people who become focused on their relationships with things tend to do so at the expense of their relationships with other people.

Of all the relationships that really helped people to overcome their sense of alienation to the flats they lived in, it was gender that turned out to be the most important. Single men, without female support, were typically the ones who had done practically nothing to change the flat over thirteen years. They had simply repainted back the original schema. But single women without male support were not in a much better state. Talking of support does not imply the kind of feminist-inspired support, where men start to help in traditionally female tasks. It reflected the maintenance of a very strict and traditional division of labour, where women are held responsible for knowing about, being interested in, and supplying an aesthetic sense of how the place should look, while in this conservative working-class arena men were expected to have no interest at all in any such issues of style. Instead men should cultivate an expertise with a DIY (do-it-yourself) tool set. A real man was a man with a power drill, the most conspicuously gendered object in the home. There is an obvious historical context to all this. Men who had traditionally spent rather more time at work in manual labour were facing a gradual reduction in working hours. This gave them more leisure time at home. But at home they were most likely to feel bored, or that they were getting under the feet of the females of the house. The rise of DIY in effect saved men's sense of their own masculinity and gave them an appropriate role within the house.

Without the aesthetic direction of women, men felt they could do nothing. Without the manual labour of men, women felt they could do nothing. But when they were prepared to exchange these skills, the result was a transformation of the kitchen that represents their combined efforts to overcome the initial state of alienation from the state. Sometimes the results were quite extreme, with Tudor-like half-timbering crossing over the ceiling; or absolutely everything from tiles to dishwashers in shades of blue. In such cases the couple had appropriated the original state fitments and personalized them so they could now identify positively with their own dwelling. Or at the extreme had thrown out the original fitments and purchased their own.

This conclusion suggested that two things that could easily have been studied in isolation really needed to be considered in relation to each other. On the one hand, there is the way the relationship to wider powers of the state and the market gives rise to a condition of alienation. On the other hand, to understand which households were able to overcome that condition of alienation, we have to examine more intimate relationships of gender. Stuff, in this case in the form of kitchens and their decoration, was integral to the way these two sets of relationship interconnect. Curiously, what emerged from this study of kitchens was a relationship of reciprocal exchange between males and females that looked for all the world like that which the anthropologist Marilyn Strathern had seen as the core to Melanesian societies in her book *The*

Gender of the Gift.[3] Strathern had used her Melanesian studies to argue that gender was not a given; gender studies should not be studies of what men do or what women do. Rather creating differences, that in turn create the conditions for exchange, ultimately creates what we recognize as gender. Making the transformation of the kitchen dependent upon an exchange of women's aesthetic concerns with male manual labour reinforced a clear definition of gender itself.

This account is highly generalized. Not every couple works things out in this way. Quite often couples originally form on the basis of the attraction between highly gendered individuals; a macho man being attracted to a conspicuously feminine woman and vice versa. When they become a couple living together, the opposition, which was once a source of mutual attraction, may or may not be reconciled in their development of their joint home. They may find a negotiated compromise. So, in one case, a woman gets the bedroom as her nest, evident in the luxurious bed with a teddy bear in the middle. Meanwhile the man can control the living room and populate it with computer games and a chair that takes a can of beer in the armrest while he is watching football on TV. Another couple may have a horror of what they regard as such gender stereotypes and strive for equality and sharing. This will produce a rather different, more compromised, aesthetic.

But often a woman's desire for equality is thwarted by larger power relations. As in the case of the kitchens, we may want to focus upon personal relationships, but find there constant echoes of much wider struggles of power. The problem for Georgina is that her husband is a professional artist with strong views on art and many other aesthetic matters. As a result, Georgina finds considerable difficulties in dealing with the aesthetics of the home, or trying to make it a medium for expressing their relationship. She is well aware that this activity of decoration could and should include far more compromise and shared projects than are likely to emerge within a sphere where his opinions are so clear and strong. She would have liked to include some romantic pictures, but he is tending towards minimalism. As a result, there are simply no decorations on the wall at all. Georgina knows full well that if the house has now emerged as a mirror of her social relationships, it throws into relief mainly their incompatibilities. Better to leave it be.

A final example comes from a year's study carried out with Zuzana Búriková on the experience of Slovak au pairs in London.[4] When we started to look closely at the rooms which host families allocated and prepared for their au pairs to live in, it wasn't long before a clear pattern emerged. It seems that most families didn't think twice before deciding that IKEA represented the perfect source of au pair style. Not just IKEA in general, but specifically white melamine IKEA furniture, which was found in approximately half of the photo-documented au pairs' rooms we studied.

The reason lies surely in the very direct analogy these families see between their understanding of the au pair and their understanding of IKEA. Just like the au pair herself, white melamine from IKEA is generally seen as inexpensive, generically European in a young, modern poise, characterized by cleanliness, functionality and efficiency. Hopefully reasonably long-lasting, and quite easy to replace. When there is a change of au pair, the slate is wiped clean and one can begin again with the blank white surface, the impression of the previous occupant removed more or less instantly. In general the au pairs themselves are perfectly happy with the result. Such rooms are clean, easy to tidy, functional, modern, and bright. In Slovakia IKEA is considered somewhat upmarket. Somewhat bizarrely for a firm based in Sweden, but much of whose furniture is actually produced in Eastern Europe, many of these same items cost more in the Slovakian IKEA than in the IKEA in London. Only later on do many au pairs start to perceive another side to this functional modernism, its coldness and anonymity.

In all these cases the home has been used to bring into focus issues of power that were deliberately kept out of focus when discussing clothing. But there are reasons why each genre serves its respective illustrative purpose. Houses, the elephants of stuff, attract the attention of power, in a way that clothing, dismissed as mere trivia, mainly doesn't, but of course sometimes does. But we have also started to domesticate the concept of objectification itself. In the case of the kitchens it would be as true to say that the homes are tools for the construction of gender as to say it is men and women who combine to appropriate homes. Modernism creates design, but the middle class discover their own values through suburban design used as a bulwark against modernism. These stories are certainly about housing, but look beneath the surface and they remain also stories about objectification.

Home and Agency[5]

Many social science approaches seem to imply that, unless their analysis is all about these kinds of power relations, they have failed in their political duty. But the analysis of power relations, just as that of social relations, can easily decline into a kind of mechanical reductionism. The last chapter tried to show how a theory of objectification implies contradiction as intrinsic to culture. Such contradictions are not necessarily and not merely a reflection of these other relationships. So it is useful to examine also cases which are not necessarily about power and oppression. Instead perhaps we should turn to someone who is really rather fortunate. Who has had the ability to choose for himself pretty much exactly the house he would wish to occupy and who, with a decent salary and good fortune, has the means to cultivate a relationship to a house and home relatively free of the forces so far discussed. Take, for example, the author.

I have been more than a little fortunate when it comes to house buying, starting with our very first house in Manchester, for which my wife and I paid out the princely sum of £19,000. Mainly by dint of prices rising at the right time and place, we progressed from those beginnings in Manchester to my present London home which is well beyond any house I had ever expected to be able to occupy, especially in terms of style. I am not well versed in the arts and I don't have a lot of respect for my taste in such matters (nor does anyone else). However, I have always had a fondness for the arts and crafts period, ranging from jewellery by Archibald Knox to the architecture of Charles Rennie Mackintosh, which in the UK is a pretty commonplace affection. My house was built in 1906 and is quite unusual in that none of the rooms is a simple square. It also, in the immortal words of all estate agents, 'retains many original features' ranging from the oak staircase to various fireplaces and their surrounds. So, OK, the circular roses on the stained glass windows are not actually Mackintosh, but they are clearly sub-sub Mackintosh, and that's good enough for me.

I am fortunate then in occupying that typically English idyll of suburban house and garden. Indeed I am writing this in a study at home looking out on squirrels, jays, foxes and blue tits. There is, however, one, I would admit relatively slight, problematic feature with this tiny tale of suburban bliss. The house is just a bit too good-looking, too close to the style I hugely admire, but could never hope to emulate. The problem is that, as any householders, we have to paint walls, choose carpets, add furnishings, put up curtains and so forth. And speaking for myself (not, I hasten to add, the rest of my family, whose tastes are impeccable) I constantly feel that anything I choose to do will fail to live up to the standards set by the house itself. Ideally I would buy and place things that complement and complete this aesthetic I admire. But inevitably, when I have chosen a cushion cover, when I have placed a new piece of furniture (some of these are from IKEA) I feel instead that I have betrayed and demeaned the house that really deserves someone with better taste than myself. I have not just let myself down; more importantly I have let my house down. I simply don't possess taste that equates with its original aesthetic.

Obviously I am not in any way trying to equate my good fortune, in living within an aesthetic that I perceive as superior to myself, with the plight of people forced to live within often soulless estates about which they had no choice whatsoever. I am contrasting, rather than equating, my position with this largely powerless population. The point is that, even when there are no such external or oppressive conditions, it does not therefore follow that we are returned to some idealized version of the theory presented in the last chapter. There are a wide range of reasons why people might not feel that the house is simply a vehicle by which they are positively constructed and developed. My alienation from the house derives solely from my sense of inferiority to the house itself.

In the last chapter it was suggested that we can find, within the myths, rituals and cosmologies of peoples in Melanesia or Australasia, evidence for the contradictions of objectification appropriate to their circumstance. Starting from my individual point of alienation, we can generalize this to English people as a whole by examining our own forms of myth. Take, for example, the genre of haunted houses. If we think for a moment of the classic haunted house, it is very unlikely that we have in mind just some very ordinary terraced property in a London street. If a property such as mine was really lucky, it might just manage to get itself a poltergeist, but it's most unlikely to attract a fully fledged ghost. For that honour we probably need to inhabit some ancestral pile that has been standing for generations and inherited its ghost from a tragic death, several centuries past; the little girl in blond ringlets who hid in a clothes chest and was never able to get out again, or a gallant knight who took his own life on hearing of his lover's demise.

My personal favourite within the genre is fictional, *The Canterville Ghost* by Oscar Wilde. The two key factors in this tale are first that it concerns an old house with its own name and history. The second is that the purchaser, Hiram B. Otis, was an American with little disposition to mind such things. Hiram B. Otis, who proclaims that he comes from a modern country, shows no respect for the well-established ghost. The first action by the new mistress of the house is to attempt to remove (with the assistance of Pinkerton's Champion Stain Remover) the bloodstains of Lady Eleanore de Canterville, murdered there by her husband in 1575. In subsequent pages the distinguished ghost becomes horrified by the materialism of Otis and his children's lack of respect for a pedigree such as he possesses and his many past achievements in the honourable act of haunting. To cut a short story very much shorter, it all ends well, of course. The ghost is finally laid to rest in the garden of death, as Otis's daughter, having fallen in love with the Duke of Cheshire, comes to respect and assist the historical tradition represented by the house.

The association of ghosts with stately homes is hardly an invention of Wilde. Basically the older the house the more chance that it is haunted. Very commonly the ghost gives evidence for aspects of the history of the house that were otherwise unknown, for example, a priest's hiding hole, or a lost hall or room. Ghosts clearly have a marked tendency to cling to their old haunts. Why, though, should the new owners of such houses find themselves encumbered with *possessions* beyond those they had knowingly purchased? The reason is that these ghosts are expressing precisely the theoretical point being made by our dialectical theory. They are even closer to what was introduced as alternative attempts to transcend the opposition of subjects and objects: theories

associated with writers such as Latour and Gell, who talk in terms
of the agency of things. That is, we think that we, human subjects,
are free agents who can do this or that to the material culture we
possess. But inevitably we can't. Objects can be obdurate little
beasts, that fall from the mantelpiece and break, that refuse to
grow in shady spots in the garden, that cause us to trip, and that
crash their systems just as we were about to type something genuinely interesting. If, in all such cases, they are clearly not reflecting
the agency that is represented by us, then it seems reasonable to
start talking in terms of the agency represented by them – the
gremlins. In short, one way of thinking about these theories of
dialectics, or mutual constitution, is to imagine material culture
as having agency all of its own. Things do things to us, and not
just the things we want them to do.

This was the point I was making about my own house.
Theoretically I own the house, and I should be able to do any
damn thing I want to it, subject only to the feelings of my family
and the laws of the state. But of course I can't. The wretched house
is simply too good-looking and constantly humiliates me. But as
long as I am prepared to be humble and respect its original features, I gain a great deal of pleasure from it. This is partly also a
condition of my understanding that the house was built in 1906,
had many occupants before me, and may have many after me.
Compared to it I am quite transient. This is still more evident if
one is living in some stately home built centuries ago. Then, the
current householder may feel more like someone keeping it well
for the future, rather than simply being the owner. We have a
sense that the house has its own powers and properties that lie
beyond us – something that may be easier to comprehend if we
give that power and history an anthropomorphic form. Instead of
saying that the house has agency, it is easier if we stick with the
entities we normally think of as having agency, namely people,
even if, in this case, they are dead people. A ghost may express
this feeling that there is power in the mere longevity of the house,
an agency which represents the limits of our own agency. A ghost
can stand for that ancient history in a manner that we cannot.
Or, to put it succinctly, perhaps we should realize that ghosts are
the original *estate agents* (sorry!).

It is not surprising that this point about the sometimes obdurate
nature of material things uses the example of the house rather

than that of clothing. A house is much more likely to be experienced as an independent and autonomous agency than some lesser species of material culture. But the basic idea that things have agency holds for much more flimsy substances. Keane makes the point very effectively through an ethnographic study on the island of Sumba in Indonesia.[6] One of his key examples is that of a piece of cloth that is torn when being transported by one group of people to another. No one intended the cloth to be torn, but inevitably people will interpret the fact that it was torn as significant. It may well be seen as a sign of undeclared agency of a person, such as a hidden reluctance to give the cloth, or it may be the agency of malevolent spirits as opposed to humans, intervening to ensure this less satisfactory outcome. What the haunted house story shows is that people in England, as well as in Sumba, conceive of spirits who pre-empt our modern theorization of agency as a possession of stuff.

Of course most of us do not live in haunted houses and our strategies for dealing with the temporality of our homes are usually rather more mundane; however, they can still make manifest some stark contradictions. There are two main ways people generally work with the longevity of their homes when it comes to furnishing. One group tends to prefer genuine antiques, sometimes only those of the period of the home itself. Others respond by purchasing reproduction furniture. While some people combine these, quite often there is considerable antagonism and disdain between the two camps. For those who prefer reproduction items, true antiques may be seen as 'coffins' of furniture. The idea that people had died in that particular bed make it, for them, something to be avoided at all costs. For the buyer of antiques, the purchase of reproduction furniture is viewed as fundamentally dishonest. Those people are thought of as cheating, betraying the proper search for authenticity. By contrast, for people who buy reproduction furniture it is the purchasers of antiques who are dishonest since it is reproduction furniture that is being clear about these being contemporary additions to the site, since the antiques didn't actually come from or with that particular property. The debates go on beyond mere purchase. Does the inglenook fireplace have to be where it would originally have been or can it be made from a conversion of a space under the stairs? Or do you go so far as to renovate the house itself with antiquated methods such as oak beams with oak pegs?

Such contradictions are not a feature of the relationship of housing to the state and forms of power, but something intrinsic to certain properties of materiality, in this case longevity. We are forced into taking positions on wider cosmological issues of authenticity, truth and identity. This is all part of our need to come to terms with the agency of stuff itself. A useful way of thinking about this, in respect to housing, is to reflect upon the various meanings of the word *accommodating*. On the one hand it speaks to the need we all have, to find accommodation in the sense of a place to live, and accommodation can cover many such spaces, from the homes we might own, to temporary rented forms such as student accommodation. Secondly, this may also involve a process of accommodating in the sense of an appropriation of the home by its inhabitants. Less obvious is that this second meaning is reciprocal. It may imply our changing of a home to suit ourselves, but it can also imply the need to change ourselves in order to suit our accommodation. Thirdly, the term accommodating expresses a sense of willing, of benign agreement to compromise on behalf of the other, often the only spirit within which accommodation can be achieved. By considering our relationship to the home through the term accommodating we face the home not as a thing but as a process. Being accommodating and being accommodated is something with which we are constantly engaged. So how, then, does accommodation become accommodating? How do we, in practice, achieve this balance between our agency and that of the home? To explore this further, it helps if we split the problem up into a series of different registers or scales of accommodation. Fortunately this can be exemplified by a series of research projects that were carried out by some more of my then PhD students. While none of them was conceived with this sequence in mind, on juxtaposing them, they form a rather useful sequence. Each represents a different stage and scale in the study of the dynamics of accommodating.

A project by Jean-Sébastien Marcoux examined the process of moving home in a site, Montreal, where this is done frequently and often on one particular day in the year.[7] Marcoux notes that we start with many assumptions about moving house. It is supposed to be traumatic, destabilizing and even a cause of ill health.

But his study tries to examine why people might often move for what they experience as quite positive reasons. Moving house allows for a kind of critical realignment of persons with their possessions. When moving house they discard some of their stuff but, in contrast to the house itself, many other possessions move with them. As such, moving house allows people to reconstruct their personal biography as represented in memories of associated objects and thereby the sense the family has of itself. Certain relationships with other people get discarded along with the objects that memorialized them, while others come to the fore and are used prominently in the decoration of the new home. So people have a chance to, as it were, work on and repair the way they represent themselves and their own histories to themselves, and to the world, in accordance with how they now want to see themselves. He concludes that moving home is a way of rewriting one's autobiography, inscribed in things.

Moving down the scale, Alison Clarke (who also shared the shopping fieldwork with me) looked at changes that take place through the refurbishment of rooms within the home.[8] This is an activity subject to its own simplistic and generalized clichés, mainly about 'keeping up with the Joneses', which view interior decoration as a site of aspiration based on emulation of one's neighbours. In the context of a rise of privatized and more materialistic lifestyles, this is the image most journalists have of home decoration. Clarke replaces this cliché with a far more informed and complex understanding of what the house performs in mediating the relationship to others. The context for her studies, that of working-class households within British state housing, presents an initial paradox. On the one hand, there is a clear concern with neighbours, 'the Joneses', and with what other people might think about one's home. But, in accordance with British working-class historical traditions, there is almost no actual visiting of homes by neighbours (visiting is almost exclusively by kin). Such families never actually see their neighbours' homes, so who exactly are they emulating?

What Clarke discovered is that, in practice, the key relationship was to the home itself, rather than to neighbours. People feel more the discrepancy between the actual home they live in and the images they possess of aspirational or ideal homes, derived from various sources. Take, for example, an immigrant's aspirations towards assimilation or, the opposite, a chance to reconstruct one's ethnicity. Alternatively the aspirations of a single woman towards the place she will live in with her ideal partner, or her aspirations for the future of their children. It is the home itself that is used to objectify such goals: to create an imagined environment that achieves integration, or stands for some future state. The home as a mirror of aspirations also becomes a battlefield for the individual or couple as to whether they are living up to, or betraying, their own ideals. In short, we find they constantly judge themselves against the representation of who else they might be, as constructed by the refurbishment of their own homes.

Sometimes the ideal home is held as an external myth, and most ordinary actual homes betray a very different set of relationships. In a study called 'the untidy Japanese house' Inge Daniels shows, from her evidence living in a series of Japanese homes,[9] that actually these are quite different from the external portrayal of such homes as a kind of natural and immaculate minimalism – the kind of Japanese homes portrayed in Sunday newspaper supplements in the UK. Actual Japanese homes bear little relationship to the Japanese home of our Orientalist projections. Furthermore, there is a deeper significance to the fact that most homes tend in practice to be quite untidy. This is equally true of the nature of the Japanese family and domestic relationships within the home, which also have tended to be portrayed in overly tidy and clear categories.

Finally, this use of movement and change in the process of accommodation can be taken all the way down to the smallest scale. This became evident to Pauline Garvey while researching in a town in the south of Norway.[10] Because she was present as an ethnographer, she saw not only the major changes that take place in the home, but the little movements, such as putting a chair or table in a slightly different position within a room. In itself trivial, but when seen over the longer term, such actions have two important consequences. Partly they bear on the horror people have of the idea that they are nowadays stuck in a rut, that nothing is ever going to change. Households may not want to have to contend with things that are significantly different. The chair might be put back the way it always was, after a while. But at least the inhabitants have expressed their agency over that of other persons and things. They can demonstrate to themselves that they still retain a capacity for change. Secondly, these are in effect small experiments, ways of re-thinking how things could be, different configurations, that mostly will not amount to anything, but occasionally become the catalyst for more significant changes in the environment within which people live.

Each of these studies illustrates the process of accommodating as an example of objectification. In no case are people merely representing themselves in their homes as a static relationship. In each research project it is the dynamics of the home that is paramount, whether moving house, refurbishing a home, creating mess or merely moving stuff around. In each case the persons are once again creating themselves through the medium of stuff. The problem with such examples, as so often with material culture studies, is that they can feel relatively trivial, of limited consequence. We have travelled some distance from power and ideology in order not to be overwhelmed and reduced. But throughout this chapter there has been an insistence that the little details and the grand ideologies are usually linked. So the final example returns to global issues, in this case migration, but seen through these intricate details of home decoration.

Caribbean Homes

People don't just move homes, sometimes they move countries, and this brings into focus the potential gulf between home and homeland. The starting point for this example is the initial phase prior to such separations. Here we can reprise some of the earlier themes about how homes objectify values, before following the migration to London. The perspective then splits to examine, first, some of those who remain in London, and then those who become return migrants. The examples are taken from the two islands in which I have carried out fieldwork, Trinidad and Jamaica. In the case of Trinidad, the fieldwork has been intermittent over the course of twenty years.[11] It started with a year living in the town of Chaguanas, near the centre of the island. But I was not the first to write about this town. It was the birthplace of the novelist V. S. Naipaul and the setting of several of his best-known novels, of which many would consider the finest of all to be the felicitously named *A House for Mr Biswas*.

Chaguanas is not exactly a tourist destination and, as it happens, one of the very few houses that remain from an earlier period, and has any sort of character, is the very house which was the setting for that particular story.

I have always been in awe of this superb novel that, with a poignancy I couldn't hope to even begin to convey, manages to capture one of the central arguments of this book, and I am sure was one of my inspirations. The theme of the novel is an increasingly desperate desire for objectification through one's own home. It concerns the poignancy of failure, of the pathetic nature of these attempts to objectify, when seen through the lens of a frustrated life, with limited resources and an unkind fate. The tragic failure that haunts Biswas comes from living in a succession of houses that he does not own and on which he leaves little mark. Without a house of one's own it was impossible to imagine a family and especially a descent line. The prologue ends with these sentiments:

> But bigger than them all was this house, his house. How terrible it would have been, at this time, to be without it: to have died among the Tulsis, . . . to have left Shamas and the children among them in one room; to have lived without even attempting to lay claim to one's portion of the earth; to have lived and died as one had been born, unnecessary and unaccommodated.[12]

Though fiction, Naipaul's book gives this abstract theme character and significance, and provides the perfect illustration of the points made in this chapter. Eventually Biswas does end up with a property, a ramshackle affair, jerry-built for a quick profit, full of faked and insubstantial elements, but a property nonetheless.

By the time I arrived in Chaguanas in 1987 Trinidad had experienced an oil boom, and the generation that followed Biswas had opportunities to fulfil these dreams and took them. I worked with four communities, based on a relatively wealthy residential area, a government housing sector, a village incorporated into the town and a squatters' camp on the periphery of the town. Amongst other studies I took around 800 photographs from 128 living rooms, for analysis. The remarkable quality of these living rooms was their homogeneity. The furnishings within them, often sofas and armchairs, tended to be upholstered either in maroon or in brown, and these colours were picked up by many of the other associated objects such as curtains, carpets and possessions. Most comprised a standard set of items such as the *space saver* – a set of open shelves, filled with ornaments, that does more or less the opposite of what its name implies. There would usually also be present a *buffet* (glass cabinet with kitchen and other wares), homilies often with religious ideals, artificial plastic flowers and stuffed animals or dolls, often still in their dusty plastic bags or boxes.

The subjects of decoration were most commonly fake tapestries of coniferous woodlands of the kind that would never grow in Trinidad. Religious themes such as the Last Supper were also common, as were items pertaining to mothers or Mother's Day, and weddings. I was never quite certain if the merchants holding or swigging tankards of beer were Portuguese or Dutch. The single most common motif was swans, perched in every kind of concrete, plastic, wood and stone, though I don't think I ever glimpsed the bird itself in Trinidad. Overall this characterization was regardless of income level or residential area. So, for example, both wealthy and impoverished Trinidadians collected quantities of cheap ceramic ornaments.

There are some clear themes in these interiors: the preference for artificial things, for filling up spaces, content that is orientated to family, religion and education. Above all, a layering and covering of things, from the crochet-style toilet roll covers to *throws* (cloth that covers the sofa seats so that you don't actually see them) but also the fact that the stuffed toys remain in their plastic bags, or that artificial lace covers a variety of different surfaces. It is not hard to see wider social values inscribed in these things. Complementing covering and layering are certain rituals for piercing these layers. For example, one of the most elaborated layers is the very professional cake decorations. The occasions when these are ceremonially cut with a knife are also about the only time when it is acceptable to kiss in public. This and several other examples start to suggest a more general opposition between sexuality, with its potential for uncovering and exposure, on the one hand, and this aesthetic of layering and covering. The filling of the living room with its layers and lace, the wedding photos and the educational certificates on the walls, all speak to the project of family longevity and respectability: exactly the values which are threatened by sexuality, associated with the outside and the street, the ever present threat of disruptive bacchanal introduced in chapter 1.

This spills over to genres other than the house itself. Inspired by Naipaul, the intention had been to work on the home, but once in Chaguanas it was impossible to avoid noticing how much this town was dominated by the car, the concern of 38 of the 176 commercial establishments in the area where I lived. There were garages and car part specialists, but they were dwarfed by three stores devoted to car upholstery, whose owners became wealthy enough to own much of the area's commercial property. Apart from domestic upholstery at Christmas, the trade was largely car upholstery, and the three major firms merely dominated a host of smaller car upholstery firms, making this probably the leading commercial concern of the town.

During this fieldwork, which took place during the recession period of the 1980s, upholstery was dominated by repairs to vehicles such as taxis. But during the previous oil boom most new cars had their first outing to these upholsterers, who could transform everything from the car seat to the trunk (car boot) with designs such as fake snake skin or a black leatherette streaked bluish and silver, marketed under the title 'New York by Night'. Even the dashboard could be upholstered, cushions added, and the whole complemented by a variety of paraphernalia such as perfumes, religious icons and stickers. Cars could also be feminized, for example with heart-shaped satin cushions with projecting pink frills and central flower designs. The degree of such personalization was satirized by a journalist who recorded his removal of the accretions to his new second-hand car:

> The tiger-skin covers came off on day one, as did the red plastic steering wheel cover; as did the little duckie. The white JPS emblems made it to day two, but no further; nor did the 'I love my Mazda' sticker. Presently slated for retirement are: the dashboard heart that lights up in red with the words *love caressing*; the pair of little green bordello cabin lights; the red hyphen lights above the front number plate; the fog lights inscribed Denji; and at least one of the three antennae.[13]

The commercial centrality of car upholstery made a bit more sense in the light of people's more general relationship to cars, which went well beyond anything one can experience in London. This was partly economic, what is locally called *pulling bull*, whereby non-commercially registered cars are actually used for taxi work. But the intimacy with cars went way beyond instrumentality. In Trinidad individuals may be located as often through the car parked in front of a house as by their house number. The local press constantly spread scandal and innuendo through reference to car ownership as in 'The leader has a nickname which resembles that of a popular large local fruit, and he drives a taxi which is neither too dark nor too light',[14] or it might talk of an AIDS victim 'whose husband drives a Mazda'. Retailers, irrespective of what they were selling, routinely decided their expectations of particular customers entering their shop on the basis of their car, and so I would be told that a Laurel driver bought this, but a Cressida driver would not buy that. Occasionally people knew of another individual by their number plate but not their name. Trinidadians would queue in cars rather than walk the last few metres to deliver a child to school and would stay within their car while the child played in the park. A car owner would shudder in horror when a passenger slammed the car door too hard, and, when home, carefully cleaned the tread within the tyres.

If the upholsterers were devoted to car interiors, there were other shops in the same high streets who would foster equal care for the car exterior, tinting the window glass, adding stripes to the exterior paintwork or ensuring the car was up to date with current fashion by replacing metallic wheel hubs with white. On closer inspection it seemed that this division into two genres of car beauty products reflected two distinct groups of customers. As with so many dualisms in Trinidad, these are presented first in terms of ethnic stereotypes. A conversation described the Indian with gold on his fingers and hair greased back who wanted crushed velvet upholstery but could only afford short-pile acrylic so he spent ages brushing it the right way. By contrast, there was the Black dude, ideally with his *deputy* (mistress), though the tinted glass ensured that at least you think she might be there, projecting the person through the car thanks to the external paintwork and the very loud sound system.

In material culture analysis, one set of stylistic forms starts to make sense when it can be seen as consistent with others. The dominance of upholsterers suggested they had other interiors to transform as well as the car. An obvious extension is the home interior. Here too one saw material covered over by layers, but the values being expressed were also clearer. Less obvious was the link to the funeral parlours. But they also turned out to be a major outlet for upholstery since coffins, and the more expensive and luxurious caskets, are almost invariably lined in deep buttoned upholstery. Putting together the aesthetics of home, car and coffins started to account for the significance of upholsterers. The transformation of the car interior turned it into a vehicle not just in the sense of transporting people, but also a vehicle for transporting values. Specifically the values of the home interior: long-term family values. Values that could be continued aesthetically even after death and through death. In stark contrast the shops devoted solely to the car exterior suggested the car also served as a vehicle for the individualism and mobility associated with the world outside the home.

From this vantage point we can see how a town dominated by the upholstery industry gives us insights into larger contradictions of Trinidadian society. On the one hand, it highlighted an orientation to family, to long-term reputation, to the past and tradition, to accumulation including education that gives solidity to the family. This cluster of values can be termed *transcendence*. They contrasted systematically to a constellation of values which can be called *transience*, the same values discussed in relation to style in chapter 1, expressing an always ephemeral and temporary achievement of freedom. An identity created in the moment of performance.

This in turn explained the way Trinidadian life is pivoted around two key festivals. Home decoration is central to the celebration of Christmas. Much of Christmas ritual consists of buying things for the living room, emptying it, tidying it, and ending Christmas Eve with the ceremonial re-hanging of the curtains that enclose it and constitute it as a given space. Even the street-wise young men, who live the life of transience, find that at Christmas time they have to locate themselves in the nexus of family, and help with the home decorations. One of my favourite fieldwork moments came when a man used me as an excuse to avoid helping his wife with Christmas domestic chores, and drove me to the house of his *deputy* (mistress) where he spent the evening – carrying out Christmas domestic chores for his deputy, of course.

If there is a systematic contrast between Christmas and Carnival, then there is also a remarkably clear point of transition. This takes place on 'Old Year's Night' (New Year's Eve), which starts with the most important Church service of the year and ends with the most important party of the year. So the study of stuff, and the patterns of what people do with stuff, is probably as much effective at revealing the underlying structural tension that objectifies Trinidadian culture order as anything Trinidadians might say about themselves. The reason an individual, such as Naipaul's Biswas, is so driven to achieve a life through taking possession of a home is because the home is foundational to objectifying that set of Trinidadian values with which he identifies. But if Naipaul brilliantly conveys the Caribbean aspiration to being accommodated, in contemporary Trinidad this tension is most eloquently expressed by that heavily upholstered living room on wheels that we call a car: that same population on the one hand wants to retain those family values, but on the other is also increasingly tempted by the allure of the car's mobility and its promise of freedom from the home and family.

This analysis of house and car illustrates the way material culture is studied as the objectification of values. But it remains an ethnographically based, static portrayal. From this starting point we can take off, as did so many Trinidadians, and travel in time and space to Trinidadians as migrants to London from the 1950s onwards. Not surprisingly, we find in London a dynamic synthesis of the two regions, to the extent that, within a generation, young people are quite uncertain as to what derives from where. For example, many younger Londoners of Caribbean origin think of the living room or front room as a kind of sacred space, a place they would be often banned from, except on Sundays. This owes little, though, to anything Caribbean, but owes much to working-class British traditions. In their search for respectability in London the migrants had copied the tradition of the parlour, a sphere of respectability, hardly used at all, outside of Christmas or for very special visitors.

Home interiors pay little heed to whether their contents relate to any particular tradition. An exhibition recalling the home interiors of immigration juxtaposes reggae with Jim Reeves, souvenirs

of St Lucia with souvenirs of the British seaside.[15] Today there is
a fashion for roots: the idea that if migrants remain true to their
older traditions it may give them strength in resisting the racism
and oppression they confront through the migration process.
Actually this is highly unlikely, and one of the portraits in the
book *The Comfort of Things* provides a clear example of why.[16]
The values that maintain respectability within the extended family
of Caribbean traditions may just result in loneliness and the
appearance of aloofness in London. What we call roots are likely
to be part of the integrity of one kind of life. If people want to
protect something of that life, it is likely that a creative synthesis
sensitive to the change of context is going to be more effective
than pure conservation or some model imposed by a state.

The world, however, is not so liberal and the end point of this
story, so far, comes when some of these same Caribbean migrants,
faced with problems such as racism in London, decide to return
to the Caribbean. Or they simply follow their original intention,
which is often to return to their place of origin on retirement.
Here I am indebted to Heather Horst, whose PhD concerned
the homes of those migrants who had returned from the UK to
Jamaica.[17] When her work is published I hope it will have as a
frontispiece one of the graves she showed me in rural central
Jamaica. The grave in question took the form of a rather dinky
looking miniature concrete house, complete with doors, windows
and gables. It looked more like something to put dolls inside than
a corpse beneath. Some of these graves are surrounded by the style
of ironwork identical to that which surrounds actual houses. She
interprets these graves as marking the end of a long journey home,
aspired to in life, but only achieved in death.

For most Jamaicans the project of building a house is not a
one-off, single act. Most people could only afford to build their
own house in stages. As money accumulated, one might lay a
foundation for a new room, or complete the tiling of another.
Building the home was a life's work and in turn became the
primary mode by which life itself was marked as a progression.
Despite all the pressure from the church, it was not having
children that led people to marry; it was the ability to have some
sort of house of one's own. This close association between life
and building a home is obviously complicated when a Jamaican
migrates to London. Most Jamaicans, given the nature of colonial

education and governance, had come to regard Britain as a kind of second home, a source of their own cultural identity. In practice they experienced in Britain a sometimes violent repudiation of what they had seen as their own British identity.

In many cases this reinforced the initial intention of returning to Jamaica on retirement. Well over twenty thousand returnees have made this trip. But once they do return they face a second, even more unexpected, rejection. In general Horst found that the tendency was to migrate, not back to their original district of origin, but to an upland, relatively cool area of central Jamaica that seems somehow more English. Furthermore, over the decades of exile the migrants have developed an affection for certain elements of English life, such as an English-style garden. In turn it emerged that those who remained behind saw these returned migrants as indeed principally English rather than Jamaican. They worried that returnees with greater wealth would lay claim to land and authority at their expense. So ironically the people who had failed to become English through migration to England found that the moment they finally achieved this goal was when it was no longer desired. Many felt they were no more at home in Jamaica than they were in London.

If they could not create a home through a sense of homeland, it was once again the house they sought to transform into home. One of the principal incentives behind the initial migration was to earn the kind of salary that would build the house they had failed to construct on local incomes. These settlements in upland central Jamaica are full of such houses: houses whose scale and style are instantly recognized not as Jamaican, but as 'returnee' houses. Faced with this initial failure to become Jamaican again, Horst observed that many of these returned migrants increasingly spent their time going to, or being involved in, the organization of what become highly elaborate funerals. It was only in death, interred in the earth itself, beneath these miniature models of the perfect house, that the final return to Jamaica was successfully completed. A return blessed by deep religious faith in another final return to another heavenly place of origin.

These graves are the end point of a chapter that began with a discussion of modernism as ideology in the history of London housing. A chapter intended to exemplify the consequences of the theoretical ideas elaborated in the previous chapter. The result, I hope, is an absolute mess. We start trying to move into a nice, neat, newly built theory – minimalist and austere. The pure dialectic, in which we finally appreciate that subjects and objects exist only through the process of objectification in which each constitutes the other. An absolute theory that will give us mastery over explanation and understanding. The problem is that, as soon as we tried to furnish our theory with examples, they turned the whole thing upside down. The case studies now lie strewn higgledy piggledy all over the place.

Actually the theory is still there if you look hard enough. Whether it's Mr Biswas, Georgina, the Slovakian au pair in London, or the Caribbean migrants. Everyone is trying to engage in being accommodating as well as in being accommodated. They are all trying to find themselves, root themselves, create family descent or just a decent household through the stuff that is the home. The home is indeed a powerful instrument of objectification. But it is very rarely either a simple, let alone a heroic achievement. Hardly ever is the result a clear reflection of the intentions of the human actor. The process of accommodating is battered by floods of other factors: the agency of the house itself, haunted or otherwise, the dictates of the state, the profession of architecture, the limits of resources, the arguments between couples, the refusal of people to accept you back as Jamaican, the superiority of one's own house to one's own aesthetics, the contradictions of real antiques and reproduction furniture, the attempt to adhere to roots that betray you.

So the house as a form of objectification draws us into a maelstrom of power and instructional interests that often make us feel comparatively powerless. But to acknowledge these forces – governments, peer pressures, asymmetries of power by gender and class – doesn't mean that we now see people as their passive victims. We have witnessed all sorts of creative responses to these onslaughts. Often expressed in material objects, such as in the suburban rejection of modernism, cramming spaces with personal ornaments, or simply ignoring the local council and knocking down an interior wall.

House interiors are often a mess because the compromises that we constantly have to make with authority add to the compromises that result from another of the critical components of our dialectical theory: the centrality of contradiction to culture.

Trinidad is not to be understood as one overwhelming set of values, but rather as a constant tension between diametrically opposed values. London is neither modernist nor suburban, but a tension between these two. Just as the relationship between an individual's aspirations and the collectivity represented by talking in terms of the collective word *Trinidadian* is an irresolvable tension, so it is not surprising that in surveying actual homes and houses, we often find scenarios that are tragic, pathetic, or unresolved except through death. However, as made clear in the book *The Comfort of Things* they most often emerge as some kind of expressive logic that does indeed objectify their inhabitants, which in the circumstance is some kind of triumph.

One more conclusion follows.[18] Except for the very first example of modernism and suburbia as façades, all the evidence for this chapter depends on a willingness to step inside the private domain of other people. To study stuff, we need ourselves to be where stuff is. Right there, in the living room, the bathroom, the bedroom and the kitchen. This is where most of modern life is lived. Families are created in bedrooms and sometimes divorced there. Memories and aspirations are laid out in photographs and furniture. Yes, peering into the wardrobe you may be accused of voyeurism, of a lack of respect for privacy. But actually most people would face their anthropologist in the kitchen rather than standing on the doorstep with pen and clipboard. So if you spot stray, bedraggled anthropologists, out in the rain, looking for a dry living room to conduct research in – be kind – give them a cup of tea and they will listen to you all day and pay more respect to your choice of wallpaper than you could ever have guessed.

4

Media: Immaterial Culture and Applied Anthropology

There is no point just adding media to clothes and houses. For starters, the media is rather less obviously a material thing, and is better addressed as a form of technology. There will also be some mention of commerce, which has been rather ignored so far, though this topic is mainly left to the companion volume *Consumed by Doubt*. But perhaps most importantly, I haven't so far asked why all this matters – beyond the intellectual curiosity of academics. Can such studies also lead to an attempt to intervene, advise and take responsibility for these new understandings? Is there a potential for research in material culture to contribute to the welfare of populations? Basically, can we start to make ourselves a bit useful? So this chapter ends on a more applied note concerned with the insights the study of stuff can contribute to the alleviation of poverty.

But we start with the technology. What kind of stuff is communication technology? For example, we may decide we want to initiate a discussion of the Internet, but what is the Internet?[1] Using the word Internet we may forget the constantly changing configuration of things that people do online. The early genres of Internet use that were associated with activities such as *flaming* have pretty much disappeared. Today there are some regions where people know nothing about surfing for information and see the Internet as a place for chat, while in other regions they surf but don't chat. The Internet is not a thing, and has no clear material form except through the box and screen that is the computer. The Internet is not one of its particular usages. Rather it's a term we use to consolidate genres of usage that are linked through online access. Should the Internet be regarded then in terms of the capacities that seem inherent in it, in its actual usage, or perhaps the way it is understood – what we gloss as its meaning, when we use the term Internet?

Even the physical link to the computer quickly breaks down. This association works in many countries, but when studying in Jamaica it soon became obvious that almost no low-income families could afford computers, so the very idea of chatting online, or surfing, was primarily seen as an attribute of the mobile phone. For people such as myself, used to keyboards, chatting by thumb looks remarkably clunky. But these Jamaicans simply did not see their Internet phones in these relative terms. They just saw the excitement of their first chat room on a mobile phone, their first music download, and all sorts of obscure information. The weather forecast in Jamaica, New York, has surely never before been quite so exciting.

We might feel more comfortable turning to the idea of inherent usage. Here the evidence from Jamaica points in the opposite direction, because I had really no appreciation of what the inherent usage of the mobile phone was until I went to work there.[2] In London, while nearly everyone has a mobile phone, for most it is just an instrument for making phone calls. Others, usually far fewer than those desired by phone companies, take an interest in the phones' built-in capacity to surf the Internet, or to send videos. By contrast, in Jamaica, many people who have mobiles have ceased to wear a watch. Why bother when a phone can tell the time and sound an alarm? With a much greater facility for appreciating the advantages of *free stuff*, Jamaicans seize upon a multitude of secondary features. A phone is a handy calculator, quite often a diary and calendar and certainly the principal means of storing contacts and one's personal social network. It can record short memos to help in micro-management of work or personal affairs. Children play games as one would find in London. But it was in Jamaica that one could find people hand-crafting hardcore pornography, pixel by pixel, that could be sent by phone, though the results impressed more through their ingenuity than their realism.

Many Jamaicans travel with their mobiles in the palm of their hand. Some exploit it as fashion, changing the fascia to match their clothes. Many women much prefer little pink clamshell phones. They might also do this in London, but there is no one in my neighbourhood similar to that shopkeeper in Kingston who routinely stores her phone within her ample cleavage. Men too, as one put it, may want 'the wickedest phone, the blingest phone'. Schoolchildren can match style so that they can 'look girlfriend and boyfriend through their phones'.

Then there are ringtones which effectively dress the phone. Religious Christians, for example, often use common hymns and religious music to make their phones more appropriate. My favourite was an aspiring preacher who, without a trace of irony, included the tune 'Oh God you are the only one, that's why I am holding on so long'. The facility to assign ringtones to particular callers also appeals to those whose phone usage is dominated by keeping different relationships apart. Some even try to match the tone to what they see as the character of the caller, such as a 'sour' tune for a persistent ex-boyfriend. Jamaicans were equally adept at the performative potential for speaking on the phone. A young man on a crowded bus sitting with a female companion on either side of him receives a call from yet another woman. He talks as loudly as possible, drawing attention to his three women and celebrating the increasing annoyance and jealousy of one of the women sitting next to him who is poking him in the ribs and trying to get him to stop. When a man in a bar receives a call he may decide to stay in the bar because he wants people to hear the conversation, go outside because he wants them not to hear, or go outside because he wants them to think he has something that he does not want them to hear.

So the problem with the idea of inherent capacity is that usually we don't know what this is until it is manifested in usage and meaning. We know of many cases, such as texting, where something was built in as a capacity but the cultural genres it gave birth to were never anticipated by its designers. In the Philippines a relationship is not really a relationship without between 20 and 120 texts a day; this isn't an inherent capacity, but then it's not really a Filipino tradition either. It's something new. Texting has profoundly transformed what it means to be Filipino, because it has become pretty much the dominant practice of waking hours and redefined what relationships are.

So is there a more sophisticated way to see these ideas of usage and capacities and technologies?[3] Anthropology can contribute its own understanding of what we mean by technology, if we are prepared to see mobile phones on a par with the way Trobriand Islanders use spells to grow crops in their gardens. Based on his reflections on a book by Malinowski called *Coral Gardens and their Magic*,[4] Alfred Gell wrote an influential article entitled 'The Technology of Enchantment and the Enchantment of Technology' that was a precursor to his wonderful book *Art and Agency*.[5] It's an approach that is particularly well suited to topics such as the Internet and phone. He noted that if you are interested in the technology of, say, an animal trap, this has to be designed around the shape, but also the behaviour, of the particular animal you have in mind to trap. For example, if you want to trap me, I recommend chocolate.

The Internet is best seen not as technology but as a platform which enables people to create technologies, and these in turn are designed for particular functions. So what people weave from the fibres of the Internet are the traps they use to catch particular kinds of passing surfers. They require a design that draws interest, attention and appreciation and thereby seduces its particular victims. When I first started looking at Internet websites I noticed that there was one genre that was particularly crude and ugly. These were the websites of Trinidadian wholesalers. Yet it is in this very ugliness that we can see the workings of the technology. When websites were first being developed in Trinidad, one problem was that something which goes on the web could potentially be seen by anyone. But if you are a wholesaler, getting the attention of individual consumers is going to be a huge waste of time. If possible it is much better to put them off. By contrast, the lack of styling sends a message they want to get across to retailers, who are their audiences, that money is not wasted on such fripperies. Rather this will be the cheapest source of the goods in question. The trap is designed to catch and hold fast those retailer animals, and not any other.

At the opposite end of the spectrum are a set of websites that are positively baroque in their ornamentation. As soon as you go on the site you are assailed with the sound of MP3s, as music is one of the most important aspects of their decoration. But then there is a blaze of colour, not still, but shifting as things pop up, open out, invite, surprise and joke around with the viewer. Somewhere beneath all this may lie a photograph or portrait that reveals an otherwise possibly quite shy schoolgirl or schoolboy, because these are the websites that circulated, prior to social networking sites, as the personal websites of adolescents. In this case they were in fierce competition, not to sell something, but to demonstrate, in this vicarious fashion, how attractive the individual was and how popular they could be amongst their peers. So the key function of the site was a section at the base that asked anyone visiting the site to sign on at the end and make a comment. This created a visual demonstration of just how many people had been attracted enough to post something on their site, as against horrible Charlene, who occupied the next desk and would never, and should never, be quite as popular, even on the Internet. Today this has been taken over by social networking. You just have to have more friends on Facebook than your mates. You also have to have a photo taken of you clutching your handbag, mascara running, asleep in the corridor of your student hostel, when you were too drunk to make it back to your room. Because otherwise you simply haven't been to Uni.

So we have quickly moved from thinking of technologies of communication as merely things, or capacities, and started to see them more as analogous with the arts of seduction: ways of making ourselves appear attractive to the person we are communicating with. Obviously seduction is only one of many things going on here. The larger point is that communication technologies are essentially cultural genres and we can best appreciate them in much the same way as other cultural genres. This brings us back to our consistent theme, that a material culture approach is defined by this dialectic of mutual creation. We cannot simply ask, as most people might enquire, 'How do Trinidadians use the Internet or how do Jamaicans use the phone?' because such phrasing implies that one end of this equation, the people, is a fixed entity. A Trinidadian who uses the Internet is at least, in some small measure, a different kind of entity than a Trinidadian who doesn't. This may even amount to a change in what we mean more generically when we use the general term *Trinidadian*. A cultural genre is something that we can appreciate makes Trinidadians what they are just as much as making the Trinidadian Internet what it is. In the next section we will explore another unexpected analogy in order to appreciate what we might mean by this phrase cultural genre. When the Internet first appeared, but had developed sufficiently for us to at least have a go at trying to work out what kind of animal we were dealing with, I worked with Don Slater on a wide range of genres of usage to see which would best help us comprehend it. Surprisingly we found that the most effective way of appreciating what the Internet had already become was through our study of Internet use in Trinidadian religion.[6]

Making Trinidadians on a Wing and a Prayer

As a means to summarize our findings on how the Internet had changed people's lives in Trinidad, we proposed four main modes of transformation. When a new medium arrives on the scene, the first and most important impact tends not to be anything which is itself radically new. Rather the tendency is to seize upon it in order to finally realize some desire that was already present, but so far had been frustrated, because people didn't have the means to fulfil it. For example, the Hindu community in Trinidad had seen itself as potentially a significant part of the global Hindu diaspora, but had felt itself to be very much on the periphery of this growing community. The Internet was seized upon as a means to assert a greater presence. Similarly many Christians wished to be part of the diocese of the Cathedral in Port of Spain, the capital of Trinidad, but often they lived too far away, or even abroad. Using the Internet they could become much more actively involved in this specific site. In each of these cases the people concerned had already formulated their desires, but prior to this moment they hadn't had the means to realize that sense of themselves. So finally, thanks to the Internet, I can achieve my previously thwarted goal of becoming – me. This is usually the first consequence of any new technology viewed as a cultural genre.

In the second instance we looked at the way new media creates both new freedoms but also the need for new controls. For example, the Catholic Church has a traditional hierarchy, so that the word of the Pope filtered down to the population through various intermediary positions such as bishops and priests. With the arrival of the Internet a lay individual gains direct and instant access to the centre without these intermediaries. Similarly young Muslim women could challenge the authority of a local imam over, for example, what they were and were not allowed to do as part of their wedding, by looking at discussions posted on the web. So traditional structures and hierarchies were under challenge. But at the same time few of those who formed such religious organizations wanted these to disintegrate. So a Pentecostal site first welcomed the ability of anyone to post ideas and commentary on their site, but later insisted these were filtered through the 'elders'.

The classic tale of this contradiction between freedom and control has become an essay called 'A Rape in Cyberspace' by Dibbell.[7] He tells of how the Internet was first seen by Californian users as a welcome liberation from all authority. It represented a place where people could choose to become whoever they wished to be, often in the form of avatars, that is, online aspects of themselves, an idea that has since become more familiar with the rise of *Second Life*. But then the users studied by Dibbell found that a rogue member had worked out how to take control of other people's avatars and was making them do 'unspeakable' things to each other. Suddenly all these newly liberated Californians were casting about desperately for some version of the Internet police. This, then, is the second consequence of a new technology. We explore new things we can do, experienced often as new freedoms, but that also induces anxieties that we retain some control over how these freedoms and capacities are employed.

In our third model of Internet use, we examined the way the media is seen to mediate. For example, a group of Catholic Charismatics, situated on different islands, had developed a form of 'spiritual journeying' in which they helped each other deepen their exploration of their faith. As one woman noted, the Internet helped hugely. First, there was the advantage for women generally in that they felt liberated from having to concern themselves with their physical appearance. But more profound was the timescale of the Internet. Previously they had used letters but, by the time a reply had been received to some discussion, people had usually moved on from the position they were exploring when they first sent the letter. By contrast, in face to face dialogue people feel pressured to respond immediately, without having sufficient time to reflect upon what were experienced as very deep matters. The Internet seemed to allow, for the first time, an appropriate time-scale. One could receive a message, ponder and reflect until a response had been properly formulated and then send this within a timeframe that still represented an active dialogue.

Religion also allowed people to consider explicitly the material-ity of the media as mediation. For example, these same Catholics created a lively debate as to whether the Internet could be used as a medium of confession. Some reasoned that, even within the church, there was a screen between confessor and penitent, so that this seemed to suggest that the Internet had a clear precedent and was appropriate. However, others reasoned that the priest still had to be present to give absolution, so that one could not employ the Internet for this process. So the very specific quality of this medium, its various forms of materiality, were of considerable significance to people who constantly debated these same issues as an integral part of their religious commitment. In this third instance we acknowledge the specific materiality of the medium and the impact that has on the communication it mediates.

The first model suggests that the initial use of the Internet is based on the fulfilment of prior desires. Clearly, however, the Internet can also create new, unprecedented imaginations, thoughts that had been barely conceivable prior to this technological pos-sibility. This was clearest in the case of an Apostolic Church, partly because it fitted with the foundational theology of this church. When faced with the Internet, this church had one basic question. Why had God created the Internet at this time? Because for them, nothing that happened in the world was without divine significance. There was always God's purpose to be discerned. Mostly they reasoned that the church was designed to spread 'the word' and that all new developments were intended to facilitate that command. So previously, having seen how successful capital-ism appeared to be in the world, they had tried to use that as their model for how their church should appear, as a kind of entrepre-neurship. Now with the appearance of the Internet they believed that God had invented this thing at this time, basically for them. The only question was what exactly God was thinking of in choosing to do this right now. So, within a short time, they restyled their church *The World Breakthrough Network*. They largely abandoned traditional church services based on face to face community, and developed as an Internet-based church with Internet services. The most important aspect of the web was the way it facilitated international and global connectivity, and this was seen by the church as a sure sign that in a short while their message would become a global message. Thanks to the Internet they would thereby finally fulfil their purpose to establish God's plan for the whole planet.

These four processes illustrate what people can become through the Internet, or, in the terms of this volume, the nature of the Internet as a form of objectification. At first they strive largely to become the selves they hadn't previously been able to achieve. Later, they gain a new imagination of themselves as people whom previously they were not aware they even could become. Each of these processes comes with its own contradictions, most fully noted in those between freedom and constraint, but present in all cases. So the idea that objectification creates both its subject and its object here looks more concrete. It's not that Trinidadians use the Internet, or that the Internet creates Trinidadians. It's more that the Trinidadian Internet is something distinct from all other Internets and makes the Trinidadian who uses the Internet something beyond previous forms of being Trinidadian. There are new relationships, new aspirations and new idioms as well as new technologies.

To talk in terms of a new kind of Trinidadian cannot be reduced to the transformation of an individual Trinidadian. It implicates the very meaning of the word Trinidadian. Sometimes the capacity of the media actually to become the form by which people reflect back on who they are becomes quite explicit. To appreciate this, we can turn from this concern with new media to study a rather older medium, television.[8] During the time of my earliest research in Trinidad, by far the most popular television programme was an imported US soap opera called *The Young and the Restless*. There are many soap operas shown in Trinidad, and when *The Young and the Restless* was introduced as a daily lunch-hour soap, it was not expected to have the same importance as established serials such as *Dynasty* and *Dallas*. But Trinidadians showed considerable ingenuity in arranging to see the show. There was a big trade in imported miniature televisions which can be set up in shops and offices. Those living in a squatting community without water or electricity would have a car battery recharged weekly to power the television in their home. I couldn't help studying the soap, since I found that for an hour a day no one would speak to me. I was reduced to studying them watching it. Friends who worked as seamstresses had to watch the show to find out what new clothing their clients were about to order.

One of the most intriguing findings was the way the soap opera was referred to and used in daily conversation. Anthropologists will listen out for wise old adages and sayings that seem to capture a certain sense of cultural expectation. But it was at those times when you would anticipate some such traditional saying that typically one would hear comments about the soap such as:

'The same thing you see on the show will happen here, you see the wife blackmailing the husband or the other way around, I was telling my sister-in-law, Liana in the picture, just like some bacchanal woman.'

'I believe marriage should be 50–50 not 30–70. The woman have to be strong, she have to believe in her vows no matter what . . . that make me remember *The Young and the Restless*, Nicky want her marriage to work but Victor is in love with somebody else, but she still holding on.'

[as in a then current story] 'You always go back to the first person you loved, in my own family my elder sister went with a Muslim boy, and so was married off by parents to a Hindu man, but she left her husband, gone back to the first man and had a child by him.'

In Trinidad contemporary commentary is dominated by the songs that calypsonians bring out for Carnival, and, true to form in that year, a singer called Contender gave the reasons for the soap opera's success in the chorus of a calypso with the same title, whose content was largely a summary of the plot. The chorus alternated:

'You talk of *commess*
check the young and restless,'

with the words,

'They like the bacchanal
they like the confusion.'

If one asks Trinidadians to summarize their country in one word, the likelihood is the response will be *bacchanal*. The term has a specific meaning in Trinidad, although, as elsewhere, it evokes the values celebrated in Carnival; that is, the general heightening of excitement, disorder and expressive sexuality. It is the same spirit that motivates the *Jouvert* ritual that was discussed in relation to Trinidad style in chapter 1. The idea is that people reveal themselves in the first light as the 'truth' by their satirical exposures of the pretensions of established order. The point previously established against our concept of superficiality was that truth should be on the surface where people can see it. The first synonym for *bacchanal* is clearly 'scandal', with lyrics such as '*Bacchanal* Woman, sweet scandal where she walks', or 'We people like scandal. We people like *bacchanal*.' Scandal again implies the bringing into light of that which others want to remain hidden. Bacchanal also connotes confusion, disorder and wildness. The two ideas are linked by the term '*commess*', which also means extreme confusion, but with connotations of it being caused by scandal.

The popularity of the soap opera makes sense in this context. Trinidad is an extraordinarily dynamic society. The oil boom gave a tremendous impetus to the growth of the middle class, to the extent that they emerged at its peak as dominant both numerically and culturally. With the recession, however, many of the more fragile pretensions of the nouveau element within this class were becoming exposed. There was a continual discourse about the financial plight that exists behind the closed doors of the home, only brought to light by events such as the cutting off of the phone through unpaid bills. Even in the suburban community, there were frequent rumours about how many properties were back in the hands of the banks or deserted by migrants to Canada. So this soap opera with its theme of scandalous revelations was not lending reassurance. The attraction of the programme was that it forced its point into the key fissure which manifested the basic contradictions of Trinidadian culture, at a time when this was especially sensitive.

This is precisely why Trinidadian television could not produce a programme of this kind. Constantly watched over, as a local product, it had to produce the respectable and serious discussions of things like problems of ministerial planning. It was left to the imported programmes to deal with these highly sensitive and difficult problems as faced in daily life. The soap opera may not have looked like Trinidad. It was made in the United States by people who had quite possibly never heard of Trinidad. But in its consumption it became more genuinely Trinidadian than anything which was locally made. Most writings on media studies tend to condemn such serials as a kind of cultural imperialism. Many Trinidadians expressed much the same view. But in this case, if one wanted to clearly establish what was generally seen by Trinidadians themselves as the essential character of being Trinidadian and addressed the most difficult local issues, the best source was this US soap opera. This goes beyond the point being made in terms of Trinidadian use of the Internet. There we saw how use of the Internet created new cultural genres that could be seen as characteristically Trinidad. But with the soap opera, we see television becoming the main medium by which the very definition of being a Trinidadian, the term *bacchanal*, becomes routinely illustrated. This may not be common, but the example shows it is certainly possible.

What is a Mobile Phone Relationship?[9]

Rather more common than this act of collective self-definition is the gradual and rather more subtle development of new forms of relationship, especially in terms of media of communication, since after all they are largely an instrument of relationships. But at least some of the same issues arise. There will always be a dialectical process such that people are simultaneously creating a relationship with each other and with the media. This issue is clarified if we try and imagine what kind of relationship could be usefully termed a 'mobile phone relationship'. For example, a brother and sister living in London may develop a multifaceted relationship over fourteen years using many different media, and adopt mobile phones when they become cheap enough. This results in some minor changes, such as the micro-management of meetings in town, but these are generally insignificant when taken in the context of their relationship as a whole.

By contrast, let's hang out on a street in Manila. The Philippines established itself some years ago as the world's centre for prolific texting. Thanks to anthropological work by Raul Pertierra and others,[10] I can imagine a young woman just getting into this medium. She likes the particular way it lends itself to short, ambiguous and suggestive, as well as creative, communication. At this stage she starts a texting relationship with a man she happened to meet when he overlooked her writing a text on a crowded bus. To be honest she had no real interest at all in the man at first. She simply wanted an excuse to practise and develop this medium of texting. But one of the treats of texting was flirting, and after a while she began to enjoy his facility with flirtatious texts, and realized this was a man she had quite a bit in common with. They did meet from time to time, there was even a brief sexual relationship between them, but that didn't work out so well, and soon they resumed what basically brought them and kept them together – the joys of text.

A third example comes from our fieldwork on the mobile phone in Jamaica. A staunch Pentecostal woman loves bringing the word of Jesus to all and sundry. She also enjoys what Jamaicans call counselling, based on her conviction that she is inspired from above. A chance miscall introduces her to a teenager, whose hesitant phone manner betrayed a fragility she seizes upon to initiate a long conversation about this teenager's problems including her child's *babyfather* who had betrayed her. This depth of confession and counselling might have been difficult if they had met face to face. But the anonymity and chance of this initial encounter led to a sustained exchange, even though the cost of the calls had an impact on both their budgets.

Which of these three cases is a mobile phone relationship? Not the first, which just adds a rather inconsequential technology, of major interest to phone companies, but not much to the participants. The second case is unequivocally a Mobile Phone Relationship, as the primary concern is texting, and the other person is mostly there in order to facilitate the use of the phone. The core relationship is to texting itself. If the second case is a Mobile Phone Relationship, maybe the third is a lower-case mobile phone relationship, in that the phone doesn't constitute, but is instrumental to, the relationship. While it is tempting to concentrate on the extreme case, it is this third ambiguous example that is by far the most common.

In order to explore this further we also need to consider what we mean by a relationship. This is a topic explored in more detail in the final chapter and will re-emerge in the book *Consumed by Doubt*, since it is a theory first formulated with respect to shopping. But to summarize, I will argue that in many cases the term relationship refers to an inevitable tension between the general category that a person inhabits and the specifics of that person. In shopping we often buy things that make an actual father more like the category of *father* as we understand it, or an actual partner more like a proper *partner* as we had envisaged them.

Currently, together with Mirca Madianou of the University of Cambridge, I am carrying out a study of long-distance relationships, specifically those of separated families. We are examining the ability of particular media to sustain those relationships over time amongst Philippine and Caribbean families. Prior to this study we already possess an established literature. For example, in her book *Children of Global Migration*, Parreñas examines the consequences of contemporary Philippine migration.[11] She notes there are approximately 9 million Filipino children under eighteen with at least one parent abroad as migrant labour. This represents 27 per cent of the youth population.

The situation seems to be one of extraordinary self-sacrifice. In her sample the average mother spent only 23.9 weeks out of the last eleven years with her children. This means that these women more or less missed out entirely on their children growing up. The mothers gave their reasons for taking up this work largely in terms of the children's welfare, such as to support their education, medical bills and augment income more generally. Parreñas's reasonable expectation was that the rise of regular and cheap communication would help to ameliorate the negative consequences of this separation, and enable the children to feel close again to their mothers and to better understand and appreciate their condition. She also anticipated that they would be influenced by the more egalitarian and modernist forms of gender relations by which the father would take on more domestic roles, in recognition of the mother taking on more of the traditionally male role of the breadwinner.

However, most of the detailed description and analysis that is found in Parreñas's book suggests that these expectations are not fulfilled. The reason for this becomes much clearer in terms of the theory of relationships just described. What tends to happen is that the period of separation simply exacerbates the distinction between the idealized norms represented by mother and child, and their actual relationship, which in these cases has significantly diminished. These norms are held both individually and collectively. At a collective level, Parreñas shows there is a dismal view taken of the families where mothers have gone to work in other countries and left their children behind. These families tend to be stigmatized. There is a belief that such children, being brought up without their mothers, will behave badly. At an individual level, the greater proximity afforded by the development of mobile phones, if anything, reinforces the most conservative and traditional gender ideals about relationships and leads many of these children to concentrate less on the material benefits that accrue to them and more on their sense of abandonment by their mothers. To appreciate this failure of increased mobile phone use, we have to note that even mothers who return home more frequently are not necessarily regarded as better mothers.[12] By contrast, it is perfectly possible for absent fathers to be seen as behaving adequately, in just keeping in touch by phone, unlike mothers, because for fathers this more occasional or distant relationship is closer to the normative expectations of fathers.

We have barely started our own research on this topic and our conclusions are likely to change. I include this here to make a further point. Now we have embarked on this study we spend much of our time talking both to the mothers who have spent many years in the UK, missing out on the development of their children, and we have now also travelled to Manila to talk to children who largely grew up without the presence of their mothers. On the one hand this is a neat academic exercise. If you want to know the consequences of new media for relationships, then such an extreme case is right on the button. But to merely exploit these mothers and children to improve academic knowledge would be pretty heartless. Nearly every week I come home with stories circulating around my head that as a parent I find appalling. These mothers and children don't just talk, they convey, they conjure, they force one to acknowledge, to try and imagine, to empathize, and finally to realize how distant one remains because privilege and good fortune have meant that one listens but does not directly share their experience. Yes, I sincerely believe this work will help us understand how relationships are affected by the media. But much more than this, it tells us why we really do need to understand such things.

In fact the reasoning that led to this study was not that this was a neat academic example. It was actually sitting down and looking at the literature on migration and Diaspora, and realizing that perhaps what academia had neglected was the one thing that mattered most to the migrants, the core relationships that were sundered by becoming a migrant. There is a vast literature on labour relationships, citizenship, identity and other such subjects. But we felt that if one actually asked the migrants themselves what mattered most to them in terms of the impact of becoming a migrant, they are more likely to respond with a very different topic: their core relationships of love and obligation, exemplified by mothers separated from children. People tend to care rather more about the people they love than the definition of who exactly they are. Yet relatively few studies focus explicitly upon this dimension of migration as against fashionable topics such as identity.

Media, Poverty and Welfare

In an edited collection of the work by my PhD students called *Material Cultures*,[13] I argued that the study of material culture needed to move away from an overwhelming emphasis upon meaning, to a greater consideration of what *matters*. While some academics seem almost to prefer a clear separation between academic studies devoted to theoretical agendas, and applied academic work concerned with issues such as policy and development, I see this as exactly the kind of dualism that an extremist anthropology should seek to dissolve. I can think of no better testing ground for theory than the heat and heart of people's lives in the extremes of what we abstractly call development, but which signifies a maelstrom of transformation, struggle and aspiration. Nor is the justification for theory as a contribution to intellectual understanding in any way diminished by regarding it as a contribution to understanding and assisting in people's welfare.

Stuff matters. Its presence or absence is quite often the very definition of what people experience as poverty. It is the main reason these Filipina mothers give for working away from their children. So the final part of this chapter focuses on a study of the consequence of stuff that was motivated by these applied concerns with the welfare of low-income populations.[14] The study of mobile phones in Jamaica, carried out with Heather Horst, was funded by DFID, the British Department for International Development. The concern was to establish the impact of new media on poverty and whether this should be a priority for aid policy in the future. Unusually, since most applied topics are more short-term, the grant was made to anthropologists who were committed to carrying out a traditional ethnography. Horst spent the entire year in Jamaica, having previously worked in Jamaica on several other projects over the course of ten years. She lived six months with a family in a rural site near the centre of the island and spent a further six months living with a family in Portmore, an outer district of the capital, Kingston. Both are low-income areas with high levels of unemployment. I lived with those same families for part of the year.

The question that DFID posed at the time remains hugely important today. The mobile phone has spread at such an astonishing pace. But 2004 was probably the first opportunity to make even an initial assessment of its impact on the lowest-income groups, because it was only by then that it had spread down to that lowest-income population, both in Jamaica, and many other parts of the world. It is entirely possible that the mobile phone is a new gimmick that represents a considerable cost and ultimately a drain on these very low incomes. Alternatively, it might represent a considerable boon and genuinely new way for people to improve upon those incomes. One problem, however, is already made evident by posing the question in these terms: is income itself the best measure of people's wellbeing? One of the arguments that anthropologists, such as Mary Douglas,[15] had been waging upon those who develop measures of human welfare was with regard to the evaluation of communication in its own right. Under the influence of economists such as Amartya Sen the United Nations had been opening up its index of national wellbeing beyond the single criterion of income, to include factors such as education and health. Yet so far communication remained understood largely as a means to such ends rather than as an end in itself. Douglas, by contrast, argued that communication is such a basic human concern that it needed to be valued in its own terms. This may be particularly true for the Caribbean. Earlier anthropological studies of the region, with titles such as *The Man of*

Words in the West Indies,[16] had examined the place of performative conversation in society and showed in considerable detail the importance of the imperative to communicate. For example, in Trinidad, if you are a man standing on a street corner and a woman passes by, it is incumbent upon you to call out something to her – you just have to. So if media, as a genre of stuff, is to be made relevant to an assessment of people's welfare, it cannot be reduced to income. But to be taken seriously by economists, then its relationship to income must also be considered. So I will start with income and work outwards.

At the time of this study Jamaica was unusual in the Caribbean in terms of mobile phone impact. Unlike Trinidad, where our previous research had concentrated on the Internet, there was almost no Internet use amongst low-income populations in Jamaica. Yet by contrast there were more than three times the number of mobile phone subscribers than in Trinidad, an average of three phones per household. Many factors explain Jamaicans' preference for mobile phones over the Internet. The Jamaican government had been faster in responding to the World Bank call for liberalization of the telecoms sector. One result had been the arrival of a dynamic Irish media company, Digicel. Starting from scratch in 2001, by the end of 2004 Digicel had sold nearly 1.5 million mobile phones in Jamaica. So it might appear that the relative success of each new medium was mainly a result of actions by the state and commerce. However, our research was to reveal another story, which had to do more with people's usage of media. But first we had to tackle the agenda set by DFID.

The general assumption held by governments and economists at the time was that if the mobile phone was to be a major force for helping low-income peoples, then this would come through two main factors. The first would be in encouraging individuals to become entrepreneurs and the second in helping people to find employment. The desired outcome would be evident in a general increase in GDP. *The Economist* magazine, in particular, has tended to argue that mobile phones might deliver on these aims more effectively than the Internet, because they are relatively cheap and require fewer skills. With a mobile phone these nascent entrepreneurs would no longer need the capital required for having an office or fixed base, and could remain in contact with potential suppliers or customers at any time.

Through ethnographic observation we were able to reach conclusions which differed markedly from such assumptions and
revealed a much more complex relationship between income and
the spread of the phone. This is not to doubt that *The Economist*'s
logic works very well for some other countries, and our evidence
is specific to Jamaica. But in Jamaica the use of mobile phones to
either assist in becoming entrepreneurs or to obtain work was
decidedly rare. There was no major new spirit of enterprise based
on the phone, with two exceptions. One was the music business.
Almost half the men we knew under the age of forty did see some
new potential in playing music, hiring bands, making CDs and
somehow making it 'big' in secular or religious music. Not that
this often happened, but the aspiration was certainly there.
Another exception was the taxi-driving business, which is so
integrally linked to the phone as to form a vital part of what can
be called their communicative ecology. That is to say, one type
of communication, that of transport, is intimately linked with
another. In our rural site you could request a taxi in which you
were already a passenger to detour up the hills to what were often
remote locations. But before the phone there was no way to
summon a taxi in the first place. This matters a great deal; for
example, in relation to the impact on health care. The phone was
used less than we expected to summon doctors or nurses, but the
link to the taxi meant that one could in emergency now summon
transport to get you to a hospital.

These are exceptional cases. In general there was surprisingly
little evidence for entrepreneurial use. Similarly in relation to
obtaining employment. The general consensus was that the vast
majority of jobs were accessed through social connections and
patronage, and not through simply matching opportunity to qual-
ifications. So if we had remained focused on income generation,
then we would have concluded that the impact of mobile phones
was disappointingly slight. But step outside that frame and the
phone was found to have a major and positive impact on the
struggle for survival by the very lowest income groups in Jamaica,
fully justifying the way they prioritized the phone, even when
living in conditions of destitution.

Again we can start with income, or the lack of it. We made
very detailed investigations of the budgets of low-income families
in both rural and urban settings. We went back day after day until

we found we could actually match our data for household income with our data for household consumption, something certainly not true of official statistics about budgets. The result shocked us. So many people had effectively no income from either earnings or selling things. The only way they survived was from money that came from others; from those that *have it*. In the urban area (Kingston) 70 per cent of these low-income households received money from other family members, boyfriends and partners, *babyfathers* and friends in Jamaica and abroad. Of these households 36 per cent survived exclusively through social networks and the patronage of others.

The bottom line is that over a third of households have no income at all in the sense of anything they earn. They exist only through their ability to obtain money from others. The difference between being destitute and not being destitute is having friends or family that you can call upon in a time of need, even if it is US$1 for transport. The mobile phone is the ideal tool for a Jamaican trying to create and maintain these wider social networks which ultimately seem more reliable than a company, employer or even a parent or spouse alone. As many studies of poverty have shown, the problem is that people in such conditions are in an almost constant state of crisis posed by every new demand for funds, whether this is a school uniform for a child or filling a prescription given by a doctor. There is simply no surplus of funds available for additional or unanticipated expenditures. A great many of the short stories that punctuate our subsequent monograph on this research are demonstrations of the effectiveness of the phone in resolving these crises.

So, in response to the initial enquiry as conceived by economists, we reach a slightly perverse conclusion. Yes, the mobile phone is highly effective for ameliorating the worst forms of suffering associated with poverty. But most economists would associate the alleviation of poverty with a rise in GDP, promoted by increased entrepreneurialism. A critical point for the development of such entrepreneurialism is the accumulation of capital, at least sufficient to make a starting investment. The trouble is that the mobile phone seems to reinforce the tendency to distribute income within low-income areas from those who, at any given time, *have it* to those who *have not*. As a result, there is even less chance of an individual accumulating the kind of capital that allows them to start working as an entrepreneur. One effect of the mobile phone is to make entrepreneurship less feasible by dispersing capital downwards. A means for alleviating poverty amongst the lowest-income groups is not necessarily something that creates wealth for the country as a whole.

As anthropologists, we wanted to evaluate the impact of the phone on welfare that meant more than just economic development. Horst and myself found a local term *link-up* best described Jamaicans' most characteristic usage of the phone. *Link-up* comprises a very large number of very short conversations, in order to keep in occasional touch with the maximum number of people. The average length of a Jamaican mobile phone call was 19 seconds. Earlier anthropological research has demonstrated that Jamaicans knew of sometimes hundreds of people they would call relatives, though they might not make use of any particular connection until the need arose. I don't know anyone in the UK who could name hundreds of relatives. But the earlier anthropologists assumed this was just a feature of kinship. Halfway through our fieldwork we had one of those *eureka* moments. Instead of just asking people about their social networks, we could literally scroll through their phones and find everyone they communicated with (actually we discovered that wives were now routinely doing this to their husbands' phones). Through our analysis of the content of mobile phone address books, we found this emphasis on very extensive networks was true of all relationships, since only 15 per cent of the names in these address books were of kin, contrary to the expectations of anthropologists.

If you wish to maintain such a vast network of relationships, then short occasional calls just to keep in touch makes a good deal of sense. Mobile phone conversations in Jamaica have been pretty much stripped of the normal conventions and etiquette of conversation. There is no polite greeting, and there is often no ending at all; maybe just a word such as *alright*, or *later*. Both sides recognize the importance of keeping the call to the least cost, but see such calls as a kind of minimal unit of sociality. By minimum sociality I mean the least contact you need if you want to retain an option of making more substantial contact should the occasion arise. Think of the way people in the UK send Christmas cards to families they meet in other countries, sort of keeping things simmering on the lowest light. This may be their only communication for years. Unless they happen to visit the country, in which case these suddenly become dearest friends who spend time with each other. But something only possible if at least you send the card.

About 98 per cent of calls in Jamaica are made on the basis of pre-paid cards. The transfer of money to the *have nots* can start even at this level. When someone needs money they will phone around to see who has some at that time. But even this costs more than they have. So they may start by *begging* a phonecard. A friend may not be able to afford to help you with your kids' education, but they may not begrudge the cost of a phonecard to help you find someone who can. The phone companies had soon come to see the importance of just keeping in touch. Digicel introduced a new facility called *callme*. This allowed a person with less than JA $3 (about UK 3p) on their phone to contact up to twenty-one other persons a week in the hope that the person they were calling would agree to accept the cost of the call on their credit. Within a few short months, *callme* accounted for over 80 per cent of all text messaging.

It isn't hard to explain why people ask for a phonecard or use *callme*. Typically anthropologists would predict some kind of generalized reciprocity lies behind this, but we found this played only a minor role. True, an individual who becomes known for always using *callme*, even when they could afford to pay for the call, is soon reviled for this abuse. But, in general, people who pass on credit and money to the lowest-income individuals have no real expectation that one day they will be repaid for this, or gain something in return. These are not just kin so it is not some very long-term sense of a wider collective interest either. Yet *callme* would probably not have lasted very long if it was rarely, if ever, successful. In fact it was in constant use.

We concluded that the reason for giving a small amount of money, or credit, is really the same reason for making a small and cheap phone call. It maintains and extends this very extensive network. Again this sets us against the economists, a perspective that tends to reduce phenomena such as extensive networking to some kind of economic need. Instead we prefer to return to our earlier point about the value of communication. Yes, this is used to help people in poverty, to get in touch with taxis, to put pressure on relatives abroad to send remittances – which is now one of the main sources of income. But these extensive networks existed prior to taxis and remittances, and seem to develop irrespectively of such functions. They flourish even when there is nothing at stake except another address to put in one's phone. While networking is vital in understanding coping strategies, the implications of cause and effect could also be reversed. People give and take not because they need to do so but also in order to facilitate connectedness. They give money in order to create the connections, as much as they develop connections in order to obtain the money.

We started by looking at the economic benefits of the mobile phone, but by the end we are coming to see that economic transactions may themselves be a means to facilitate communication, which now finally emerges as an end in itself. We may not go so far as Douglas and Ney who assert 'a social being has one prime need – to communicate'.[17] But in the end we have a conclusion that justifies the inclusion of communication as a kind of stuff. The media is not merely a means to another end. People value communication in its own right as a thing they either can possess or feel bereft of. Many other sections in our book *The Cell Phone* are concerned with this wider context to communication.[18] One of the chapters is devoted to the Jamaican concept of *pressure*, familiar from the lyrics of Bob Marley. Pressure also is often linked to a feeling of loneliness and in turn to the need for communication as an end in its own right.

A problem with anthropology is that we have a tendency to end up with a story that is largely just a 'spoiler' to economics. Predictably the anthropologist informs you after a lengthy study that the whole situation is much more complex than you previously thought. Suddenly you have to deal with this thing called culture, which seems to defy economic models. Or they may tell you that if only you spend much more money on some infrastructure or concern of that population, the people would be better off. It is much easier to just be a critical anthropologist, showing all the ways development doesn't work, without taking responsibility for making feasible and costed proposals which can be subject to other people's criticisms.

I was well aware of this tradition of critical anthropology when I started our project. My hope was that we could do something quite different. We tried to make proposals which would lead to the already heavily indebted Jamaican government spending less money, rather than more. For example, showing why a huge investment to develop community computers using a large loan of aid money was not the best use of that money, since it depended upon a concept of community that was not applicable to Jamaica. Similarly there were vast sums going into IT facilities for schools, most of which were failing; that is, both the IT and the schools. Our alternatives included putting IT money into the much more motivated sector of adult education, when people who had experience of unemployment became highly committed to training. Similarly we could see scope for using mobile phones to gain access to international standards of educational material that would be more effective than the large sums going into localizing content which were not well respected. Instead we needed to develop kitemarked educational materials under the auspices of a body such as UNESCO, since, without kitemarking, people used Google and ended up with a mess of supposedly educational material some of which was useful, much of which was crap. They desperately needed help in sorting the wheat from the chaff.

So we were quite prepared to come forth with proposals that were the opposite of those associated with mere critique. Proposals that cost less and looked feasible. I really do believe that material culture has a potential role in policy and in actually improving the welfare of populations. But that is not to say that I can claim that anything I have done or proposed actually has been useful to date. As far as I could tell no one either in government in Jamaica or DFID (who funded our work) took a blind bit of notice of any of our findings. My experience has been that people working in development listen to other people working in development, people working in bureaucracy listen to other people in bureaucracy, people in social anthropology ignore other people in material culture, and so on and so forth. No doubt this is a vice I also share.

To date I know of only one single instance in which my work has been directly applied to create something in the world. Many years ago I was giving a paper in Austria, and someone came to see me afterwards and said they were delighted to meet the person who was responsible for Big Foot. I hadn't the faintest idea what they were talking about. It turns out that someone in Austria had read *Material Culture and Mass Consumption* within which they noted a paper by Alison James that I had summarized, discussing children's sweets.[19] On the basis of the logic of that argument they had devised a new ice cream in the shape of a large foot. Which at that time was selling quite well. So, much as I would like one day to concretely assist, for example, in the alleviation of poverty in the Caribbean, the only direct claim I can make so far to the practical advancement of the world is an Austrian ice cream. And even that was based on someone else's paper, that I had merely summarized in my work. Worst of all I forgot to go out and try a Big Foot, it might have been yummy.

Fortunately, though, academics don't depend entirely on direct impact. As one follows the careers of students occupied in a range of sectors from academia and commerce to planning and design, it is evident that material culture studies has become well established, and that its educational message has diffused quite widely. The results have included a more general interest in ethnography and qualitative studies in a range of fields concerned with the material world. But I would like to believe that the paramount influence has been our contribution to a significant change, evident in many professions over the last two or three decades: that groups such as designers, architects, media specialists and commercial bodies, once motivated more by prizes awarded for the quality of their products, have increasingly realized that they need to focus on something quite different. Ultimately what really matters are the consequences of those products for people.

5

Matter of Life and Death

The premise for this book has been the observation that things make people just as much as people make things. But this can either sound like a glib sound bite, or remain an abstract theoretical proposition, as presented in chapter 2, unless it is shown more clearly how precisely things do in fact make people. The starting point for giving substance to this perspective is provided by Bourdieu's observations in *Outline of a Theory of Practice*.[1] Individuals grow up to become, with varying degrees of typicality, members of a given society. This happens in most cases, not through formal education, but because they are inculcated into the general habits and dispositions of that society through the way they interact in their everyday practices with the order that is already prefigured in the objects they find around them. I live in a complex network of houses arrayed around streets, which facilitate cars. Cars are presumed not just by the roadways but by a rich paraphernalia of other devoted objects ranging from traffic lights to parking lots. I gain my understanding partly through sheer familiarity and partly through enforced consciousness when it comes to taking my driving test. Alternatively I might live in a society where I come to assume that the health of the crops I grow is dependent upon a host of spirits and ghosts from my ancestors, which I see in all the little shrines, offerings, patterns for planting crops and so forth, set up to ensure that ancestral ghosts are properly propitiated. I may be spared any formal examination but

I will learn from priests and parents and from ridicule when I get things wrong. I will know in one case when to stop at a road junction and in the other case when to mutter a spell because I am passing an inauspicious tree.

We have explored the different ways this proposition may be understood using examples from clothing, housing and the media. We have abstracted this to the highest levels of theory. It seems appropriate in a final chapter to ask, though, just how stuff contributes to the very formation and loss of a person. To see how things are used to define matters of life and death. I guess this point only really became clear to me when I read the work of Linda Layne who had carried out an extensive study of late abortions and stillbirth.[2] I had often taught the work of Mauss and the argument about how the exchange of things creates social relations. But I had never really felt the profound meaning of this, in my bones, until reading Layne. Layne showed how parents in the US dealing with late foetal loss and stillbirth insist that at Christmas time a gift is given to the person who would have been, or from the person who would have been. She tells of the trouble parents take to dispose of the layette, the things bought for the envisaged child, as part of mourning for the death of the child. The central fear of these parents is that other people will think that what they have lost was not a human being, a child, but a mere thing. The paradox is that it is primarily through material things that they find the most effective means for insisting upon the humanity of their child; that they were not just a thing. Only real people can give gifts or receive gifts. There is a poignancy to this example that helps make material culture studies more of a mission and less just a conceit. Yes, really, it is usually through the medium of things that we actually make people. In this chapter I want to confirm this point through two main case studies, that apply to people such as myself; people in London. The first will concentrate on birth and the second on death.

Birth[3]

As a middle-class, Jewish academic living in North London it is not surprising to note that I have several friends who are involved in psychoanalysis, either professionally, or as clients. I confess that while I embrace the Jewish bit, I am not of the psychoanalytical faith. I find, in comparison to anthropology, that psychoanalysis is on the one hand too universalizing with a strong essentializing tendency in the more vulgar forms, and on the other hand too focused upon individuals as against social relations. It also has an infuriating habit of using the term *object-relations* to talk about persons entirely de-contextualized from things. The only objects this phrase recognizes seem to be other persons.

Still, it seemed like an interesting experiment to juxtapose material culture perspectives on what produces people such as myself, with these psychoanalytical perspectives. Based on the little reading I have done in the area, mainly papers by Melanie Klein,[4] I came up with a joke mainly aimed at my friends working in this field. I suggested that psychoanalysis is really a huge act of projection. The stages of development described by Klein are not really about infants at all. Instead they describe the various stages which a parent goes through in order to develop as a mature parent. This is the result of collective repression in which psycho-analysts all had such problems coming to terms with parenting that they shunted all the key problems onto the infant. I do not pretend to be knowledgeable about psychoanalysis. I have read little and understood less. But based on this joke I embarked on an examination of the use of consumption in bringing up children. I wanted to show that this does help us understand something of how these two categories of the person, infants and mothers, are given shape. A further inspiration was the work of Marilyn Strathern,[5] who suggested that in Highland New Guinea it is understood that, in some sense, it is the child who grows the mother.

The research was a by-product of my study of shopping on a street in North London,[6] for which I joined a group composed largely of middle-class mothers who belonged to the NCT. Although the letters NCT stand for National Childbirth Trust, it could more appropriately have been called the Natural Childbirth Trust since at that time its most active members and literature often expressed an almost obsessive concern with the concept of nature where applied to childbirth and childcare. At the most extreme its members were attracted to semi-cultic practices such as re-birthing, where the mother is expected to relive the experience of her own birth (although such practices are formally outside of the NCT). NCT members are encouraged to avoid any kind of assistance in the birth process such as pain relief or sometimes even doctors. These are described as 'interventions'. It was axiomatically preferable for both child and mother to follow a natural birth without these intrusions. The research took place in the early 1990s when these ideals were at their most zealous. Today things have relaxed – somewhat.

In avoiding pain relief such mothers become more directly exposed to the extreme pain of childbirth. This may have assisted in the construction of childbirth as a kind of rite, whose subject is not merely the birth of a new infant, but in equal measure the birth of a new form of adult – the mother. Childbirth is after all the most literal of the *rites of passage*, rituals which are commonly associated with pain.[7] I observed that through natural childbirth these women are engaged in an act of recycling themselves to return to the world as natural.

According to Klein,[8] the starting point for infant development is the Paranoid-Schizoid position during which the infant is profoundly incapable of reconciling its experience of the *good* and *bad* breast. These represent two entirely opposed senses of the mother as the source of all positive and all negative feelings. I would argue that this is an entirely apt description of the perspectives, not of the infants, but of the newly born mothers. The goodness of the infant is intimately associated with its complete dependency upon the mother. It is regarded as helpless: the pure product of a natural birth. One of the key gestures of such births is that the newborn baby is placed immediately at the breast, preferably still covered in blood and other natural substances, that at all other times are considered dirty, but here emphasize continuity with her natural feeding of the foetus. The stress is on the infant as the biological extension of the mother. Furthermore, the NCT probably places almost as much emphasis on natural breast-feeding as on natural birth. All assistance is given to the mother who is prepared to breast-feed, and who avoids substitutes for as long as possible.

At this stage then, the mother has given birth to an infant who is perceived as largely an extension of her own biology, the main difference being its absolute purity and innocence. It represents a narcissistic version of the mother as refined and purified

of all that she feels is bad about herself. The context is important. Most of these women were influenced by first-wave feminism
in the 1970s. This gave them a strong sense of their personal
potential and the importance of autonomous development as
individuals. As students, their individuality was mainly expressed
in the formation of left-of-centre political opinions, but as their
incomes rose with employment, the emphasis turned to developing themselves as consumers and into people with taste. This
feminism equally impacted upon their relationships, with partners
seen as equal participants in growing a household income and
dual career.

In Klein's work, some of the attributes most commonly ascribed
to the new infant are rage, jealousy and above all a kind of
primitive guilt. I believe these are equally applicable to these
same mothers' attitudes to these infants.[9] Although all the emphasis has been on the perfection of this ideal and purified version
of themselves, at the same time the infant represents the total
negation of everything that they have striven for: the quest for
freedom from their own parents they developed as teenagers and
sustained through feminism. These mothers saw themselves as
the first generation able to compete with males. They felt a moral
duty to strive to fulfil the new potential that history had given
them, and their ambitions for their own careers were usually
clear and explicit.

What was therefore astonishing is the degree to which these
same mothers allowed the infant to trample on all such aspirations. The ideology that made their infant into the good breast
was based on its presentation as a pure and natural being. The
infant's constant demands were accepted as essential priorities
and it was felt that at no point should the mother's own desires
prevent them being attended to. The infant was viewed as passing
through natural stages with minimal parental 'intervention'. If
they woke frequently at night they must grow out of this natu-
rally and not be disciplined by some contrivance. There were
many versions of this devotion to the natural. Some saw daily
routine as unnatural, so feeding, sleeping and other activities
were dictated by the apparent mood of the infant. Others saw
routine as in some sense natural, and became obsessed that this
should never be varied. It's not altogether clear why allowing a
child to cry itself back to sleep is a contrivance to be avoided

and bringing the baby back to your bed is, however, natural. But then I am perhaps reflecting my memory of resentment over many disrupted nights.

The idea of the pure and natural infant was fostered also by the most popular literature on childrearing at that time: books by Penelope Leach, Hugh Jolly and others with their vulgarized 'Winnicotian' emphasis upon the mother's recognition that there are always good reasons for all actions of infants (such as crying). These reinforced the dependency of the mother on the omnipotent infant who, by prolonging breast-feeding as long as possible, again extended its ability to determine her life. The loss of freedom was extreme. Women who before frequently went out at night for entertainment refused to go out even once for more than a year after the infant's birth. Even though they may have had male partners more willing than most British males to participate in childrearing, the emphasis upon the biological and natural relationship between mother and infant in some ways reconstructed them as gendered in just the sense that they had so far struggled to oppose.

These are just some instances of the way becoming a mother was based upon the systematic negation of the mother's previous self. It seems reasonable then to imagine that the infant is seen simultaneously as good breast and bad breast: that which simultaneously seems to extend and purify her, but also to destroy her autonomy. The mother may be said to have been passing through the Paranoid-Schizoid position in that at such a time it was extremely difficult for her to consider that the source of such benign and such negative emotions can really be the same object. First sacrifice and later guilt arise as mechanisms for preventing this contradiction in coming to the fore, since they allow her to project all the negativity represented by the child back onto herself. Alternatively she may deflect her anger by projecting it onto her partner or her own parents.

According to Klein, the 'Paranoid-Schizoid position' develops into the 'Depressive position' (you have to admire her heartwarming terminology) when the infant learns to confront its realization that what previously had been clearly separated into the good and the bad are actually the attributes of the same object. Regarding this as a stage of mother development, this represents the start of a process of separation from an increasingly autonomous infant.

At this point stuff starts to play a role, for example toys, or the transitional object (e.g. smelly blanket) that another psychoanalyst, Winnicott, saw as helping the infant separate from its identity with the external world.

If the infant's relationship to stuff emerges through play, the mother's prior skills with stuff will have developed partly through shopping. Many of these mothers noted that the pleasure they had developed in buying clothes and items for themselves was transferred directly onto the infant. While in other communities mothers are concerned to get back their figures and clothing style lost in pregnancy, these mothers tended to channel their knowledge and ability as consumers into the task of shopping for the baby. In the initial phase clothing the child became an act of pure projection. If the infant had had a say in how she was dressed she might not have picked those faux peasant lace smocks. So when she does develop some sense of agency, she immediately declares war.

The first battle relates to the substances which the infant is allowed to ingest. There is no problem at first since the infants are entirely breast-fed, and initial foods are usually home-made pulp from vegetables. Soon, however, a villain appears in the form of sugar against which the mother strives to protect her child. Sugar exemplifies a battle against all sorts of additives or substances that are seen as unnatural and therefore polluting to the pure nature of the infant. I saw mothers react to their toddlers reaching for a biscuit as one might respond if the infant were about to stick its fingers into the socket of an electric plug. Inevitably the battle ends in defeat, as sooner or later the infant acquires considerable access to a wide range of biscuits, sweets, chocolates and the dreaded fizzy drinks. Gradually the baby is seen to lose its *organic* status through the ingestion of artificial substances. The battle is repeated as home-made and *healthy* foods pushed by the mother are rejected in favour of a diet of fishfingers and baked beans or, if the infant is sufficiently victorious, burgers and pizzas. Parents do not give up without a struggle, within which their concept of biology plays a major role. It is very common for such parents to insist that their infants have an allergy to anything artificial. Infants are said to come out in spots as soon as they ingest any kind of additive or the wrong E-number. If the children do not oblige (with spots) then the parents may claim that these additives cause behavioural problems, such as hyper-activity, which is a harder claim to contest.

The babies of these mothers were largely de-gendered. Their parents resented, rather than welcomed, cards and gifts in pale pink and blue. If anything their children were green: the embodiments of natural childbirth and rearing. As the infant began to develop its own agency, the parent might expend considerable effort in trying to prevent any association with gendered toys. This included trying to prevent girls from becoming particularly interested in dolls, but the greater effort was usually expended on avoiding guns, swords and other weapons. In conversation parents might tell with pride of their young sons' enjoyment of dolls. But even in this world of imagination it turned out to be pretty hard to fight against guns. Mothers almost invariably told how finally there was no point in preventing their sons having access to toy guns, since he was found to be using every household object from pens to coathangers as gun substitutes, happily shooting adults and siblings.

In the 'Depressive position' mothers gradually come to terms with the simultaneously good and bad qualities of their infant. But while there is a growing acknowledgement of the separation of the infant, there is still the desire to remain the primary source of all potential gratification for the infant. At first the child remains a narcissistic projection of the better (or idealized) aspect of the mother. As one mother noted:

> The difference is she has got a fantastic little figure and I have put on weight since having kids, and the honest thing is that I don't get so much pleasure, as I need to lose about two stone, that's the reason. Everything I look at I don't like myself in any more, but everything on her looks fantastic, so it is such a pleasure. I enjoy having a little girl for that reason.

The peasant smock gives way to a more youthful version of the mother – leggings, perhaps.

If there was one object that seemed to comprehensively spell defeat it had to be the Barbie doll. The particular significance of Barbie was evident given what has already been said about feminism and the passionate commitment to nature and the natural. The mothers do not object in principle to their infant dressing an anthropomorphic toy. This is seen as a learning and nurturing practice. But their preference would be for a figure that was both reasonably naturalistic and in many cases androgynous, such as to be suitable for both sons and daughters. Barbie, by contrast, is aggressively feminine and seems deliberately invented to anger such mothers. Not only does she represent the pre-feminist image of woman as sexualized bimbo addicted to fashion – she can't even stand up. This is a crushing defeat for parents who swore that their children would never succumb to such sexual stereotyping. Barbie is the unmitigated negation to the narcissistic projection of the infant as purified mother.

The capacity of children to establish radically opposed counter-cultures objectified in toys as vengeful insistence upon their autonomy is already well documented. Alison James's analysis of children's sweets (the true inspiration of the Big Foot ice cream) showed how these represent a systematic objectification of the adult's category of the inedible.[10] Any visit to the local sweetshop will reveal that the very first objects children buy for themselves are systematic inversions of adults' ideas about acceptable food categories. Pocket-money sweets are most often in the form of snot, poo, corpses and similar transgressive forms. In the case of sweets, we can understand the victory of the child as reflecting the early use of pocket money as an independent resource. While such sweets are very cheap, Barbie dolls and their outfits are expensive and may become relevant at an earlier age than these sweets. It is the mother who often purchased the objects she detests. Why should she acquiesce so fully in this tragic defeat for her own desires?

Barbie's victory is accomplished through her leadership of the barbarian horde of commodities. These pollute the mind with mindless consumerism. Many mothers claimed it was television advertising and similar external influences which turned their natural infant into a machine for absorbing endless quantities of garish goods. As a result, the infant becomes entranced by a world whose values are diametrically opposed to those intended by the parent. This is a world where foods are bright colours and full of artificial ingredients and additives, and where toys are equally garish, non-educational and non-functional. The toy shop as Early Learning Centre is soon replaced by Toys R Us, a site of utter revulsion to many of these mothers: a shop where there is no escape from the sense of toys as mass commodities reeking of materialism.

The poignancy of this decline derives from the fact that the corruption of the child by materialism directly invokes what the mothers see as their own major defeat in life. They recall their student life brimming with ideals and a certain purity forged out of their rejection of their own parents' values. This was followed by their decline into more materialistic concerns of home-making and self-styling prior to their re-birthing as mothers. Mothering had been intended to replace consumption as a superior form of self-construction through a new social relationship.

If it is the mother herself who buys the fifteen Barbies and the multitude of other toys that she had previously forsworn, this may be evidence that she has not changed her goal so much as developed a new strategy. Up to this time the mother had been seen as the major and the natural source of all that goes into the making of the infant. It may be that when faced with an opponent that threatens to overwhelm her, her response is to attempt to introject this enemy and make herself once again the primary source of pleasure for her child. Since she has had plenty of experience at constructing herself through commodities, it is not difficult for her to reinstate her role as the accomplished consumer, the means through which the desires of the child may be gratified, this time through the supply of commodities.

This development in mother–child relations is likely to be redolent with contradictions. This was suggested when observing one mother shopping at the local Woolworths. She had just complained to me that her daughter wanted a Barbie for her birthday, but that her daughter already had about fifty Barbies (a large exaggeration). After looking around for some time she chose a Barbie using a dustbuster. Two minutes later she remarked that she doesn't have a dustbuster herself but wants one. Just after paying she noted that she regrets buying this since it would have been better if the child's grandmother (her own mother) had bought it.

Parenting becomes a form of tragic practice, experienced as a series of inevitable defeats. Parents obsessively attempt to build dams and repair breaches through which pour the growing agency and autonomy of their infants. This sequence often continues into a much more explicit series of conflicts as the child grows into teenage life. The battleground moves to areas such as computer games, sexuality, drugs, parties and other genres of teenage life. In many of these there will be a similar tension between direct opposition or the attempt to buy back children through becoming the primary source of commodity purchase. But just as the Kleinian tradition is prepared to regard these stages as necessary steps towards the development of the mature infant, they can also be viewed as the foundation for a mature parenthood that has learnt to deal with problems of separation that are intrinsic to relationships that start with intensive identity and are supposed to end in autonomy. I may be having fun with them, but my intention is not to oppose or denigrate these stages which probably result in mature relationships as long as the constant defeats are accepted. While I have largely referred to mothers, this was my story as a parent too.

This research may be used to complement the work of Bourdieu. It makes this stock phrase about how objects make people into something we can recognize in our own lives, as well as in anthropological accounts of other societies. One of the primary aims of anthropology is comparative. But one reason for this is that it is much harder for us to appreciate the underlying and unspoken structures and processes that make us typical of our own society, until we have seen how different they are from the foundations of other people's behaviour. If we can see how yams make people, then we can see how Barbie dolls make people. Throughout this volume it has been evident that this use of material culture in the construction of self and society is nothing specific to capitalist or commercial societies. It is found in all societies. But it is not surprising that what the Kabyle do with agricultural implements we do with shopping.

Death

Stuff is as much a matter of death as it is of life and this volume concludes by turning to another study of the role of objects, again derived from fieldwork in a London street. This time, though, the research is situated in South London rather than North London. If the study of shopping was concerned with how the accumulation of things creates social relations, then the other side of this coin seemed to require a study of how we divest ourselves from things and how this assists us in dealing with the loss of relationships.[11]

As it happens, there is a well-established anthropological theory about the role of stuff in relation to death. Put simply, it has been argued that one of the problems of death is that it is often unexpected and usually unplanned. A rather disruptive property, given the social significance that we reasonably attribute to it. If you have no chance to prepare for it, it's pretty tricky to do death right, from society's point of view. The solution to this problem is, relatively speaking, to ignore the actual moment of death as representing merely the ending of the biological entity that was a life. Instead that event is used as a signal for starting to get prepared for all the feasting and all the rituals that should properly accompany a death. Some societies bury the corpse at once, and dig 'em up again, when they are ready to feast the dead (usually this ends with a secondary re-burial). In such ways the unplanned biological death is replaced by the planned social death. Now in this regard stuff is pretty useful. Because, if you can't control the way you separate from the living body, you certainly can control the way you separate from, or divest yourself from, the objects that were once associated with that living body.

There are many ways in which societies separate from stuff. Some are quite extreme. For example, the French Gypsies studied by Williams,[12] and the people of New Ireland studied by Küchler, more or less destroy everything that was once associated with the person. In the latter case they actually construct a substitute figure of the person and concentrate their ritual on the destruction and decay of this *Malanggan* as opposed to the body. 'The physical separation of body and soul is enacted analogically in performances that, step by step, undo the traces left by a person in the social matrix.'[13] These measures are so effective that there is no use made of genealogy, or of individual memory; only the general idea of an ancestor remains.

For some reason, however, these observations about using stuff to deal with death were always made about other societies, and have not been seen as particularly relevant to our own. By contrast, there are many professional bodies that deal with death in a place such as London and many psychological theories that are used in the training of those professions. All of which have managed, for one reason or another, to blithely ignore even the possibility that stuff plays a significant role in the way we too deal with death. There is literature on stuff in relation to death in our society, but it is almost all concerned with memorialization of various kinds.[14] What has been ignored is the very gradual process of divestment that may take place over many years. This allows us to return to the end of the last chapter, and the claim that the study of stuff could potentially contribute to the welfare of populations. Because when you turn from the professions and counsellors and theories that deal with death in our society and actually start to look at what most people do, in a place such as London, you suddenly find that stuff is actually very prominent indeed. Individuals, each in their own private domain, have found their own way to understand how they can use stuff in dealing with all kinds of loss.

Earlier discussions of this process took place within a period of anthropological theory dominated by functionalism. At that time it was fine to suggest that the death was potentially destructive of society and society took these measures to prevent or to repair the potential breach in the fabric of society. Societies were considered as functioning wholes that took such collective actions. Today, to call an explanation functionalist in anthropology is a bit like accusing someone of original sin. Secretly, though, I have retained an affection for functionalism, and feel that in certain cases, and this may well be one of them, it is a perfectly reasonable way to think about how societies do actually – function. It's not that I want to fetishize a thing called society. But, as it happens, many of my informants used language that came close to those functionalist anthropological theories about divesting from objects as a kind of repair mechanism that made them feel whole again in dealing with rupture and trauma.

The third portrait in *The Comfort of Things* concerns Elia, who is of Greek descent.[15] At first she can't bear to face the clothes left behind by her mother. She stores them at the base of her wardrobe. But over a period of fifteen years the way she comes to terms with these clothes and then the way she gives them to others, or sometimes wears them herself, plays a significant role in becoming reconciled to her loss. Another of our participants, Nadine, had to face the death of her young daughter in a fire in her flat, a fire which also destroyed all the photographs and household possessions associated with her daughter. Initially she couldn't bear to see any images or reminders of her daughter at all; the circumstances were too painful. She echoed the sentiment often evoked by others – what are mere things when a life has been taken away? It was in the second phase that she began to feel the loss of images and objects that could still give respect and form to the life that was lived. She started to collect, for example, books and other objects that were preserved because they had been at her daughter's school rather than at home. Without possessions she first had to accumulate before she could divest. This process of accumulation and subsequent divestment took many years, until finally the associated objects were reduced to those she could place within a briefcase, which she keeps in storage, and a single portrait on the wall. It is now important to her that these do not distract from her emphasis upon her other children.

So in London, just as much as in Melanesia, people use their divestment from things to maintain a control over the process of separation which is less violent and sudden than death itself. Since this is not socially recognized as a ritual of separation, they find their own routes to this process, and there are various ways in which it is accomplished. One of these could be called the natural *economy of relationships*. That is to say, to some degree, new relationships have a tendency to displace past ones. So the process of divesting from things after a death follows upon a pattern we have already established as a regular practice, when it comes to separating from past relationships. Recall the point made in chapter 3, based on the study of people moving homes, by Marcoux, about the positive side to house moving. Going to a new residence, leaving some things behind, provides an opportunity to, as it were, bring memory and memorialization up to date; based largely on deciding which past relationships still matter, and to what extent. 'Moving becomes a means to reshuffle relationships and memories by bringing them back into consciousness, by making them explicit and for deciding which ones to reinforce, which ones to abandon or put on hold.'[16]

We can only retain a certain number of objects as memories of ever more past relationships. The end point of this sequence was illustrated in the home of an elderly woman, Dora. We carried out an inventory of all the objects found in her living room. On reflection these turned out to be a résumé of her full life. One of the most poignant is the bright red piggy bank that today she still fills with 20p coins. When full it contains £50 which can be spent, a routine that reminds her of her origins in poverty. There is one photo of her as a little girl, which recalls a life made hard from birth when her father was gassed in the trenches in the First World War, and another photo of her as a girl guide. There is just one table inherited from her mother and, from the period when she first worked, there is her sewing machine. Then there is the decorated box and a valance from the Jewish family that ran the alteration shop where she was employed. There is a picture of the first wedding dress she made for herself, six decades ago, that sees its counterpoint in several examples of needlework from recent years.

Though she has the two engagement rings from her two marriages, few possessions remain from the first marriage which was mired in poverty; only the government condolence letter for her husband's death. From the second marriage, which took her to Portugal and Spain, she has a table, a carpet and an ornament from Portugal. She displays a photo of herself with her husband at a dinner party, another of one of his ancestors and a decorated box from his family. Following his death she left most of their lavish belongings to his family, returning to England to unpack some of those things she had saved on her own account. Of these she treasured the stylish cutlery, egg cups and silver cups from a high-class London shop. With the thrift reflected in her piggy bank, she would buy cutlery one item at a time until she reached five, when the manager would give her the sixth for free. She has a certificate from the ambulance service she worked with during the war, and a photo of the luncheon room where she worked afterwards for twenty-five years, ending with a certificate of freedom from the City of London, where this was sited. There is a picture from the 1960s when she looked really good, a photo of a close friend, a letter from Mrs Thatcher and a picture from a holiday in France. There is no reason to imagine that Dora intended this résumé effect. It is rather the result of this *economy of relationships*, such that each significant relationship, whether to persons or periods and events of her past, ultimately became reduced to just one or two objects, as other mementoes made way for other relationships. Clearly the more relationships one has lived through, the more any one relationship has to be pruned back to one or two totalizing mementoes in this thrift of memory.

Likewise, the materiality of each of the genres of material objects is often employed to determine the temporality of divestment, which can apply to relationships that have ended for various reasons, not just death. The wearing out of clothes may present a complementary contrast to the fixity of jewellery. But there are many quite subtle strategies. Lucy, for example, knows that music plays a critical role in her memory of past relationships. If need be she will play a specific track over and over again until she is completely sick of it and finds it irritating, in order to pre-empt the way it would otherwise have worked as an involuntary reminder of a relationship from which she is now trying to distance herself. One man, who had been left unexpectedly by his five-year partner, could not bear either to look at or to delete retained emails. In fact, he exploited our project to give me the emails and digital photographs in question, as a way of finally separating from such materials. I became the excuse for separation he was looking for.

A second aspect of this process of divestment returns us to my earlier theory of relationships, as including both an actual and an idealized component. In London, just as in many other areas, this process is also one in which an individual gradually transmutes into an ancestor by becoming largely remembered with respect to an idealized category. Most of the major divisions in social status and success that occur during life are entirely ignored in the relative homogeneity and equality expressed in most contemporary English grave practice. The size and quality of the gravestone tells us very little about the distinctions that pertained to the living. We replace actual hierarchy with imagined equality. Similarly *Gran* who is communicated to the grandchild is without faults and foibles, a highly idealized category, related to the stock figure of Granny often portrayed in popular media. Again material culture plays a central role in making these norms clear. The old clock or washing mangle eventually and effectively turn the deceased Gran into a kind of museum figure evocative as much of her period as of herself.

This works both individually and more generically. As we ourselves become older, we often relate more closely to the past as a category. We buy things from flea markets or antique shops that speak to this generic patina. That is, the objects were old and clearly previously used but there was no knowledge of any particular prior user.[17] Most people possess personal and specific possessions that can help develop this transition from the specific to the generic. For example, one informant has a tin box on a shelf from the First World War. It was evident that this box stood at one level for the specific ancestry of his grandparent, but at other levels it stood, first, for British history and then for history itself.

We don't expect people to keep objects pertaining to their parent's long decline through Alzheimer's or incapacitation through illness. Instead they retain a few photos from the wedding, the holidays, the moments when the relationship came closest to its ideal.[18] Deceased males are often memorialized by other males through items of technology: tools of their trade as a carpenter, their cricket bat or their best fly-fishing rod. These are objects which help fuse the memory of the specific ancestor with the idealized conceptualization of a man, especially the working man. A woman is more likely to be recalled through the tokens of her love and care that equally make her the generic woman. The same relationship to ideals in persons would be true of lost connections to places and things, as in the homeland represented by idealized souvenirs and postcard pictures rather than poverty. So people have both an economy of relationships that pares things down to a few key objects and also use this to transform the memory of that relationship from a more actual to a more idealized component.

The process also works in reverse. Just as those who have been lost become transformed into generic and idealized ancestors by those left behind, the older generation seeks to use family heirlooms as a kind of self-simplification to a few treasured states or idealized events. They hope that the objects they select will help their descendants become more as they would wish them to be. For example, religious parents may bequeath sacred objects to their children that, alongside their admonishments, attempt to secure a greater degree of religious observance amongst their descendants. This replaces a past English practice of having a stipulation in the will that allowed inheritance only if the descendant properly conformed to the wishes of the dead.

So, in this study of ordinary households in a street in South London, it appeared that, in almost every case, when people reflected on the loss of a relationship, they had somehow worked out for themselves that a process of divestment from the things associated with the lost person could play a major role in their strategies of dealing with this loss. These were largely of their own devising, making them typical of a more general argument about material culture. While this process of divestment seems obvious enough when described in this way, and I would expect almost all readers to think of examples from their own experience, it is found nowhere in the literature on how we should deal with loss or how we actually deal with loss. There is no public recognition; it does not appear in what is by now a quite voluminous literature on mourning and bereavement in our society.

In undertaking such a study of what are, in effect, random households, many of whom are immigrants to this country, there are other reasons for expecting diversity in observed practices. Nevertheless, after working with a hundred such individuals and households, it is possible to come up with generalizations about this process, such as implied by the *economy of relationships*. Similarly one can see that different material genres have different propensities to be used for longer or more transient processes of divestment. In writing these accounts of divestment the intention is not to impose such analytical generalizations as a normative model. I don't want to tell people that they should or should not use these processes of divestment in the way they respond to bereavement. We should be content that people find their own creative paths that may work best in the private anonymity of their individual and personal relationship to that loss. But just as in the last chapter there is an applied consequence to such research. The intention is not to teach ordinary people what they already appear to know, but to teach professionals that which they appear to have forgotten. Since there are many instances, for example, when people have to move to a care home or a hospice, where facilitating such a process, or making provision for such a process, would in fact help render the professions much more sensitive to that which people do for themselves. It is in this manner that such research can hope to become, not just educative, but also directly applied to the enhancement of the welfare of the population that has been researched.

Returning to less applied and more academic concerns: in reflecting on these issues of life and death we see how the study of material culture is at least as effective a route to the anthropology of relationships and the constitution or dissolving of personhood as any attempt to confront the nature of relationships directly. I don't think we would gain more or truer insights if we asked these people directly about love, or parenting, or mourning. The study of material culture appears a rather circuitous route to understanding people and relationships, but we may arrive more swiftly at our destination, and reach much further, than many more tempting and more direct paths.

Back to the Beginning

It is possible that some readers will view the contents of this book as not just an introduction to the analysis of stuff, but also a celebration. Although the companion volume will be directed to the negative implications of stuff as quantity, including issues of environmental degradation, there is nothing 'naff' about standing in awe and reverence in the face of stuff as spectacle. The extraordinary range of artefacts that we have created stands rival to nature. We feel no hesitation in celebrating the latter. There is a huge popular respect for the voice of David Attenborough directing our gaze at creatures and landscapes we could never have anticipated would one day appear in our living room. Many of us enjoy holidays snorkelling over coral reefs, luxuriating in the bright colours and myriad shapes. The boundary between this and artefacts has become quite fuzzy. Academics and office workers may enjoy long weekend walks through what we call nature, even when we know it is the product of centuries of cultivation and conflict. Culture itself has become far more democratized and I don't feel ashamed that I can feel lost in Radiohead through my iPod, indulge in a retrospective of Satyajit Ray or Akira Kurosawa at the cinema but also be dazzled by an MTV pop video of Beyoncé. I will also go and view commercial displays of stuff in the same manner that others go to art galleries: the design ideas expressed in the shop Liberty are a favourite; but also the creativity found in a market selling toys remade from cast-off drink cans in India or the Philippines. A domestic interior turns me into a sleuth examining every clue for understanding the people who have produced this gallery of images.

Academics by their profession, when they have finished gorging on colour and spectacle, expect to turn to knowledge and explanation. But this desire for learning and scholarship does not have to detract from being entranced by the aesthetic spectacle of difference. Amongst birds and insects gorgeous colours and extraordinary dances may have evolved as forms of mating. But in their diversity they transcend their cause in the same way as a 300-page descriptive novel, much of whose content, at one level, derives from a similar biological imperative. Studies termed social science have been stymied by the ambition to replicate, in the study of society, the reduction of the natural world to natural science. This book has tried to develop both interpretation and insight, but based on ethnography, which is a world apart from the replicable experiments of science. Modern attempts to create a reductionist science of stuff, whether in psychology or economics, seem inept and clumsy compared to the nuances of the actual stuff around us. What I would love to have been able to replicate in this book is something closer to what I hear in Attenborough's voice: a rapture that seems to balance perfectly his awe at what can be explained and in what transcends explanation.

This is a book then that seeks understanding and insight, but tries to avoid reductionism. It celebrates in clothing and cars, though it could have been custard, the quirky, the exuberant and the ridiculous in our passion for stuff. But it also shows how we can nevertheless seek to become philosophers of objectification who dissolve oppositions of persons and things, spies attempting to break the codes of difference and representation, and adjudicators of whether a new technology will or will not enhance the welfare of a population. The emphasis has been largely upon just one approach to material culture, although on several occasions the work of other anthropologists has been noted such as Gell, Keane and Latour, who tackle stuff in important and complementary ways.

The search for explanations of our contemporary material world has tended to revolve around the study of capitalism; systems of production and distribution that proliferate the stuff of everyday life. Yet there exist many discussions of stuff and the desire for goods set in entirely different worlds from that of modern capitalism. One of my favourite works as a student was the many-volumed *Science and Civilisation in China* by Joseph

Needham. There are constant references to details of appearance in the 'world's first novel', *The Tale of the Genji*. The Roman poet Juvenal wrote verses with vivid curses of greed and luxury. The sequel to this book will be concerned with the causes and consequences of consumption, including capitalism. Consequences such as carbon footprints, but also labour footprints, waste footprints, transport footprints, social welfare footprints. It will acknowledge the sense we have sometimes of both ourselves and our planet drowning in ever rising levels of stuff and its progeny, waste; as well as the harrowing stories that emerge from research in the Caribbean, India or the Philippines, about the sacrifices, the wretched separations, that people make, more each year, as they seek to travel from the farm and huts they were born in, to try and become, or at least hope that their children might become, masters of the metropolis. In the light of which most academics willingly snap out of the reverie of spectacle, in order to appreciate that much of human history and contemporary motivation revolves around these desires for goods and their often baleful consequences.

Chapter 2 spoke of the *humility of things*. On the one hand, material culture appears as society made tangible, the hard, strong material presence that displays itself forthrightly, such that we can't escape its presence. Now, by the end of this volume, it has become apparent how often the very opposite is the case. Our common sense about our common senses betrays us and makes unwarranted assumptions. Stuff has a quite remarkable capacity for fading from view, and becoming naturalized, taken for granted, the background or frame to our behaviour. Indeed stuff achieves its mastery of us precisely because we constantly fail to notice what it does. Things act much more commonly as analogous to the frames around paintings than as paintings themselves. They guide us towards the appropriate way to behave and remain unchallenged since we have no idea that we are being so directed. They are particularly effective during the early phases of socialization, where they stand as our teachers, mentors and gurus, leading us to become examples of a specific society, class or gender more effectively than any explicit pedagogic exhortations.

It is this subtle, largely invisible, quality of humility that explains why we have linguistics, geography and sociology, but we have never developed an academic discipline devoted to the theory, analysis and acknowledgement of material culture. In some ways that has been rather a good thing. This volume is not intended to help found a discipline of stuff. The tendency of academic disciplines to become disciplinarian is too strong. I tend to avoid debates about 'how anthropological is it?' or 'is it sufficiently anthropological?', collaborating just as happily with geographers and sociologists as fellow anthropologists. Without a clear discipline academics concerned with material culture have been really rather free in our ability to roam the world and consider why some things matter, when and to whom; and why people claim that the things which we have argued are most important to them actually don't matter at all.

As an anthropologist my method could best be described as ethnographic involvement intended to lead to empathy; the desire to see things from other people's points of view. But I guess, at the end of my quest, I have become not just empathetic to people, but even empathetic to the things themselves. To feel rather sorry for the way ordinary stuff has been neglected and pushed to one side by more aggressive, forthright and self-regarding media, such as language and art, and the way things are constantly humiliated as the mere symbolic representation of persons and society. Because denigrating material things, and pushing them down, is one of the main ways we raise ourselves up onto apparent pedestals. From this height we make claims to a spirituality entirely divorced from our own materiality and the materiality of the world we live within. I am not sure about a spirituality that is obtained by ideals of purity and separation, or that enlightenment is reached through a denial of the material.

I remain, as I began, an extremist. I may sit in front of a computer and conjure abstractions of theory and analysis. But then, after a while, I can't wait to take these theoretical abstractions and plunge them back into the fray of everyday life and the glorious mess of contradiction and ambivalence that is found there. My greatest admiration and respect is reserved for the ethics of pragmatism and compromise, forged amidst the ramshackle maze of stuff we live amongst. I do not seek for purity and principle. I certainly don't wish to place stuff itself on a pedestal, to ignore the harm it can cause us, or to demean our humanity. What this volume asks for is merely a consideration of things commensurate with the place they evidently have in our lives.

Notes

Prologue: My Life as an Extremist

1 All references are to my own work, unless another author is specified. In this case, D. Miller and C. Tilley (eds), *Ideology, Power and Prehistory* (Cambridge: Cambridge University Press, 1984).
2 For example, Judy Attfield's *Wild Things* (Oxford: Berg, 1992) is a textbook on material culture written from the perspective of design studies.
3 S. Hugh-Jones, 'Yesterday's Luxuries, Tomorrow's Necessities: Business and Barter in Northwest Amazonia', in C. Humphrey and S. Hugh-Jones (eds), *Barter, Exchange and Value* (Cambridge: Cambridge University Press, 1992), pp. 42–74.

Chapter 1   Why Clothing is not Superficial

1 Influential examples at that time included R. Barthes, *Système de la mode* (Paris: Editions du Seuil, 1967); M. Douglas and B. Isherwood, *The World of Goods* (London: Allen Lane, 1978); and M. Sahlins, *Culture and Practical Reason* (Chicago: University of Chicago Press, 1976).
2 The next section is based on 'Style and Ontology in Trinidad', in J. Friedman (ed.), *Consumption and Identity* (Amsterdam: Harwood, 1994), pp. 71–96; and *Modernity – An Ethnographic Approach: Dualism and Mass Consumption in Trinidad* (Oxford: Berg, 1994).

3   A. C. Carmichael, *Domestic Manners and Social Condition of the White, Colored, and Negro Population on the West Indies* (New York: Negro University Press, 1833), p. 75.

4   M. Freilich, 'Cultural Diversity among Trinidadian Peasants', PhD diss., Columbia University, p. 73.

5   H. Gates, *The Signifying Monkey* (Oxford: Oxford University Press, 1988).

6   T. Morrison, *Beloved* (New York: Knopf, 1987), p. 162.

7   M. O'Hanlon, *Reading the Skin: Adornment, Display and Society among the Wahgi* (London: British Museum Publications, 1989); M. Strathern, 'The Self in Self-decoration', *Oceania*, 44 (1979), pp. 241–57.

8   The next section is based on M. Banerjee and D. Miller, *The Sari* (Oxford: Berg, 2003), esp. ch. 2, pp. 23–44.

9   *Zari* is embroidery, originally made using metal thread, usually gold-covered silver, but today mainly made with fake metal thread or plastic.

10   Banerjee and Miller, *The Sari*, p. 32.

11   D. Winnicott, *Playing and Reality* (London: Tavistock, 1971).

12   Banerjee and Miller, *The Sari*, p. 34.

13   Some of the following discussion is based on A. Clarke and D. Miller, 'Fashion and Anxiety', *Fashion Theory*, 6 (2002), pp. 191–214.

14   D. Miller and S. Woodward, 'A Manifesto for the Study of Denim', *Social Anthropology*, 15/3 (2007), pp. 325–35; see also www.ucl.ac.uk/global-denim-project.

15   S. Woodward, *Why Women Wear what they Wear* (Oxford: Berg, 2007).

16   'The Little Black Dress is the Solution. But What's the Problem?', in K. Ekstrom and H. Brembeck (eds), *Elusive Consumption* (Oxford: Berg, 2004), pp. 113–27.

17   This material comes from Clarke and Miller, 'Fashion and Anxiety', and also *A Theory of Shopping* (Cambridge: Polity, 1998).

18   R. Sennett, *The Fall of Public Man* (Cambridge: Cambridge University Press, 1976).

Chapter 2   Theories of Things

1   'Archaeology and Development', *Current Anthropology*, 21 (1980), pp. 709–26.

2   R. Keesing, *Cultural Anthropology: A Contemporary Perspective* (New York: Holt, Rinehart and Winston, 1976).

3   D. Miller and M. Spriggs, 'Ambon-Lease: A Study of Contemporary Pottery Making and its Archaeological Relevance', in M. Millett (ed.), *Pottery and the Archaeologist*, Institute of Archaeology Occasional Publications no. 4 (1979), pp. 25–34.

4   *Artefacts as Categories: A Study of Ceramic Variability in Central India* (Cambridge: Cambridge University Press, 1985).

5   Ibid., pp. 51–74.

6   None of this is quite the same as the social science theory of functionalism, for which I provide a brief defence in the final chapter.

7   e.g. M. Douglas, *Implicit Meanings: Essays in Anthropology* (London: Routledge, 1978); M. Douglas and B. Isherwood, *The World of Goods* (London: Allen Lane, 1979).

8   E. Goffman, *Frame Analysis* (Harmondsworth: Penguin, 1975).

9   E. Gombrich, *The Sense of Order* (London: Phaidon Press, 1979).

10 *Material Culture and Mass Consumption* (Oxford: Blackwell, 1987), ch. 6, pp. 85–108.

11 L. Dumont, *Homo Hierarchichus* (London: Paladin, 1972).

12 C. Lévi-Strauss, *The Way of the Masks* (Seattle: University of Washington Press, 1982).

13 The two sources I have used for Hegel are G. Hegel, *Phenomenology of Spirit* (Oxford: Oxford University Press, 1977); and G. Hegel, *The Philosophy of Right*, trans. T. Knox (Oxford: Oxford University Press, 1967). My own discussion of Hegel is taken mainly from *Material Culture and Mass Consumption*, pp. 19–33, and to a lesser extent from *The Dialectics of Shopping* (Chicago: University of Chicago Press, 2001), pp. 176–205.

14 K. Marx, *Early Writings* (Harmondsworth: Penguin, 1975), pp. 379–400. My discussion is found in *Material Culture and Mass Consumption*, pp. 34–49.

15 K. Marx, *Early Writings*, p. 329.

16 G. Simmel, *The Philosophy of Money* (London: Routledge, 1978), and G. Simmel, *The Conflict in Modern Culture and Other Essays* (New York: New York Teachers College Press, 1968). My discussion of Simmel is taken from *Material Culture and Mass Consumption*, pp. 68–82.

17 N. Munn, *The Fame of Gawa* (Cambridge: Cambridge University Press, 1986); N. Munn, 'The Transformation of Subjects into Objects in Walbiri and Pitjantjatjara Myth', in R. Berndt (ed.), *Australian Aboriginal Anthropology* (Nedlands: University of Western Australia Press, 1986), pp. 141–63; N. Munn, *Walbiri Iconography* (Ithaca, NY: Cornell University Press, 1973); N. Munn, 'Spatiotemporal Transformations of Gawa Canoes', *Journal de la Société des Océanistes*, 33 (1977), pp. 39–52. My discussion

of Munn is found in *Material Culture and Mass Consumption*, pp. 50–67.

18 The points made here derive from the work of F. Myers, in F. Myers, *Pintupi Self: Sentiment, Place and Politics among Western Desert Aborigines* (Washington: Smithsonian Institution Press, 1986); also F. Myers, 'Some Properties of Art and Culture: Ontologies of the Image and Economies of Exchange', in D. Miller (ed.), *Materiality* (Durham, NC: Duke University Press, 2005), pp. 88–117.

19 B. Malinowski, *Argonauts of the Western Pacific* (London: Routledge and Kegan Paul, 1922).

20 M. Mauss, *The Gift* (London: Cohen and West, 1954).

21 The section that follows is taken from my Editor's Introduction, in *Materiality*, pp. 1–50.

22 L. Meskell, 'Objects in the Mirror Appear Closer than they Are', in *Materiality*, pp. 51–71.

23 M. Engelke, 'Sticky Subjects and Sticky Objects: The Substance of African Christian Healing', in *Materiality*, pp. 118–39.

24 B. Maurer, 'Does Money Matter? Abstraction and Substitution in Alternative Financial Forms', in *Materiality*, pp. 140–64.

25 M. Rowlands, 'A Materialist Approach to Materiality', in *Materiality*, pp. 72–87.

26 H. Miyazaki, 'The Materiality of Finance Theory', in *Materiality*, pp. 165–81.

27 My favourite books by Latour would be B. Latour, *We Have Never Been Modern* (Hemel Hempstead: Harvester Wheatsheaf, 1993), and B. Latour, *Pandora's Hope: An Essay on the Reality of Science Studies* (Cambridge, Mass.: Harvard University Press, 1999).

28 See esp. A. Gell, *Art and Agency: An Anthropological Theory* (Oxford: Oxford University Press, 1998).

29 Examples include T. Ingold, *The Perception of the Environment* (London: Routledge, 2000), and C. Tilley, *The Phenomenology of Landscape* (Oxford: Berg, 1994).

30 E. Durkheim, *The Elementary Forms of Religious Life* (Oxford: Oxford University Press, 2001).

Chapter 3   Houses: Accommodating Theory

1 'Modernism and Suburbia as Contemporary Ideology', in D. Miller and C. Tilley (eds), *Ideology, Power and Prehistory* (Cambridge: Cambridge University Press, 1984).

2 'Appropriating the State on the Council Estate', *Man*, 23 (1988), pp. 354–72.

3 M. Strathern, *The Gender of the Gift* (Berkeley: University of California Press, 1988).

4 Z. Búriková and D. Miller, *Au Pair* (forthcoming); and Z. Búriková, 'The Embarrassment of Co-Presence: Au Pairs and their Rooms', *Home Cultures*, 3 (2005), pp. 99–122.

5 The next section combines 'Possessions', in D. Miller (ed.), *Home Possessions* (Oxford: Berg, 2001), pp. 107–21, with 'Accommodating', in C. Painter (ed.), *Contemporary Art and the Home* (Oxford: Berg, 2002), pp. 115–30.

6 W. Keane, *Signs of Recognition* (Berkeley: University of California Press, 1997).

7 J.-S. Marcoux, 'The Refurbishment of Memory', in *Home Possessions*, pp. 69–86.

8 A. Clarke, 'The Aesthetics of Social Aspiration', in *Home Possessions*, pp. 23–45.

9 I. Daniels, 'The "Untidy" House in Japan', in *Home Possessions*, pp. 201–29.

10 P. Garvey, 'Organised Disorder: Moving Furniture in Norwegian Homes', in *Home Possessions*, pp. 47–68.

11 Most of the following material is derived from *Modernity: An Ethnographic Approach* (Oxford: Berg, 1993); see also 'Migration, Material Culture and Tragedy: Four Moments in Caribbean Migration', in P. Basu and S. Coleman (eds), *Mobilities*, 3/3 (2008), pp. 397–413.

12 V. S. Naipaul, *A House for Mr Biswas* (London: André Deutsch, 1961), p. 14.

13 *Trinidad Express*, 20 Oct. 1988.

14 *The Bomb* (a weekly Trinidadian newspaper), 21 Dec. 1990.

15 M. McMillan, 'The West Indian "Front Room" in the African Diaspora', *Fashion Theory*, 7/3 (2003), pp. 397–414.

16 *The Comfort of Things* (Cambridge: Polity, 2008).

17 H. Horst, 'Back a Yaad: Constructions of Home among Jamaica's Return Migrant Community', PhD diss., University of London; H. Horst, 'A Pilgrimage Home', *Journal of Material Culture*, 9 (2004), pp. 11–26; H. Horst, 'Landscaping Englishness: The Postcolonial Predicament of Returnees in Mandeville, Jamaica', in R. Poter, D. Conway and J. Phillips (eds), *The Experience of Return Migration: Caribbean Perspectives* (Aldershot: Ashgate, 2005), pp. 207–23; and H. Horst, ' "You Can't be Two Places at Once": Rethinking Transnationalism through Jamaican Return Migration', *Identities: Global Studies in Culture and Power*, 14/1 (2007).

18 'Behind Closed Doors', in *Home Possessions*, pp. 1–22.

Chapter 4 Media: Immaterial Culture and Applied Anthropology

1 The following section is taken from D. Miller and D. Slater, *The Internet: An Ethnographic Approach* (Oxford: Berg, 2000).

2 The following section is taken from H. Horst and D. Miller, *The Cell Phone: An Anthology of Communication* (Oxford: Berg, 2006).

3 The following is taken from 'The Fame of Trinis: Websites as Traps', *Journal of Material Culture*, 5 (2000), pp. 5–24.

4 M. Malinowski, *Coral Gardens and their Magic* (Bloomington: Indiana University Press, 1935).

5 A. Gell, 'The Technology of Enchantment and the Enchantment of Technology', in J. Coote and A. Sheldon (eds), *Anthropology, Art, and Aesthetics* (Oxford: Oxford University Press, 1992), pp. 40–66.

6 The following section is taken from Miller and Slater, *The Internet*, ch. 7, pp. 173–93.

7 J. Dibbell, 'A Rape in Cyberspace', in J. Dibbell, *My Tiny Life* (New York: Owl Books, 1998).

8 The following is taken from 'The Young and the Restless in Trinidad: A Case of the Local and the Global in Mass Consumption', in R. Silverstone and E. Hirsch (eds), *Consuming Technology* (London: Routledge, 1992), pp. 163–82.

9 The following section is taken from 'What is a Mobile Phone Relationship?', in E. Alampay (ed.), *Living the Information Society in Asia* (Singapore: Institute of South East Asian Studies, 2009), pp. 24–35.

10 R. Pertierra, E. Ugarte, A. Pingol, J. Hernandez and N. Dacanay, *TXT-ING Selves: Cellphones and Philippine Modernity* (Manila: De La Salle University Press, 2002); and R. Pertierra, 'Mobile Phones, Identity and Discursive Intimacy', *Human Technology*, 1 (2005), pp. 23–44.

11 R. Parreñas, *Servants of Globalization* (Stanford, Calif.: Stanford University Press, 2001); R. Parreñas, *Children of Global Migration: Transnational Families and Gendered Woes* (Stanford, Calif.: Stanford University Press, 2005); and R. Parreñas, 'Long Distance Intimacy: Class, Gender and Intergenerational Relations between Mothers and Children in Filipino Transnational Families', *Global Networks*, 5/4 (2005), pp. 317–36.

12 Parreñas, *Children of Global Migration*, p. 129.

13 *Material Cultures* (Chicago: University of Chicago Press, 1998).

14 The following section is taken from H. Horst and D. Miller, *The Cell Phone: An Anthropology of Communication* (Oxford: Berg, 2006).

15 M. Douglas and S. Ney, 'Communication Needs of Social Beings', in M. Douglas, *Missing Persons: A Critique of Personhood in Social Sciences* (Berkeley: University of California Press, 1998), pp. 46–73.

16 R. Abrahams, *The Man-of-Words in the West Indies: Performance and the Emergence of Creole Culture* (Baltimore: Johns Hopkins University Press, 1983).

17 Douglas and Ney, 'Communication Needs', p. 46.

18 H. A. Horst and D. Miller, *The Cell Phone: An Anthropology of Communication* (Oxford: Berg, 2006).

19 A. James, 'Confections, Concoctions and Conceptions', in B. Waites, T. Bennett and G. Martin (eds), *Popular Culture: Past and Present* (London: Croom Helm, 1979), pp. 294–307.

Chapter 5   Matter of Life and Death

1 P. Bourdieu, *Outline of a Theory of Practice* (Cambridge: Cambridge University Press, 1977).

2 L. Layne, 'He was a Real Baby with Baby Things: A Material Culture Analysis of Personhood, Parenthood and Pregnancy Loss', *Journal of Material Culture*, 5 (2000), pp. 321–45; and L. Layne, *Motherhood Lost: The Cultural Construction of Miscarriage and Stillbirth in America* (New York: Routledge, 2002).

3 The following section is taken from 'How Infants Grow Mothers in North London', *Theory, Culture and Society*, 14 (1997), pp. 66–88.

4 M. Klein, *Envy and Gratitude and Other Works* (London: Delacourte Press, 1975).

5 Strathern, *Gender of the Gift*, pp. 250, 252.

6 *A Theory of Shopping* (Cambridge: Polity, 1998).

7 A. Van Gennep, *The Rites of Passage* (London: Routledge, 1977).

8 Klein, *Envy and Gratitude*, pp. 1–24.

9 See also R. Parker, *Torn into Two: Mothering and Ambivalence* (London: Virago, 1995).

10 James, 'Confections, Concoctions and Conceptions'.

11 The following is taken from D. Miller and F. Parrott, 'Loss and Material Culture in South London', *Journal of the Royal Anthropological Institute*, 15 (2009), 502–19.

12 P. Williams, *Gypsy World: The Silence of the Living and the Voices of the Dead* (Chicago: University of Chicago Press, 2003).

13 S. Küchler, *Malanggan: Art, Memory and Material Culture* (Oxford: Berg, 2002), p. 22; see also S. Küchler, 'Malanggan: Objects, Sacrifice and the Production of Memory', *American Ethnologist*, 15/4 (1998), pp. 625–37.

14 E. Hallam and J. Hockey, *Death, Memory, and Material Culture* (Oxford: Berg, 2001).

15 *The Comfort of Things*, pp. 32–45.

16 Marcoux, 'The Refurbishment of Memory', p. 83.

17 N. Gregson and L. Crewe, *Second Hand Cultures* (Oxford: Berg, 2003).

18 E. Goffman, *Gender Advertisements* (London: Macmillan, 1979).

Index